IF ATHEISM

THE FUTILE FAITH AND HOPELESS HYPOTHESES

OF DAWKINS AND CO.

BRIAN JOHNSTON

Copyright © Hayes Press 2016

Published by:

HAYES PRESS Publisher, Resources & Media,

The Barn, Flaxlands

Royal Wootton Bassett

Swindon, SN4 8DY

United Kingdom

www.hayespress.org

Brian Johnston

If you enjoy reading this book and/or others in the series, we would really appreciate it if you could just take a couple of minutes to leave a brief review where you purchased it.

CHAPTER ONE – INTRODUCTION

There's a delightful little limerick by George Gamow (a 'Big Bang' cosmologist), which goes like this:

There was a young fellow from Trinity

Who took the square root of infinity ($\sqrt{\infty}$).

But the number of digits

Gave him the fidgets;

So he dropped Maths and took up Divinity.

That interests me as I was pursuing a career in Mathematics when I had a distinct sense of God drawing me into a greater passion for still deeper truth, truth as it relates to the bigger philosophical questions, such as 'How may one satisfy oneself that God actually exists?' and 'Does this hypothesis make better sense of life as we know it'? As I write the introduction to this book, it's the season of Advent. Increasingly, western society is set on demystifying the Christmas period, majoring on replacement terminology like 'Happy Holidays', indulging in mere sentimentalism, and prefers to hang idealist hype on a 'mere winter's tale'. I like to remind friends, however, that choosing this approach has serious consequences. For one must believe in either one virgin birth or the other – and by the other virgin birth I mean the view that the universe exploded into being all by itself. Somehow, inexplicably, from a state of non-being, 'it' - something that was non-existent - exploded!

You can see how nonsensical that is, for if there was ever once truly and absolutely nothing, there could not now be a something – at least not without God (but that hypothesis is discounted). So, here's the thing - standing where we are now, as hard as it may seem to believe in the existence of God, it's even harder to believe in absolute nothing.

On the other hand, the child born to the virgin, the child who is Jesus Christ, was given a name that comes from the name by which God revealed himself to Moses: 'Yahweh' (meaning I AM who I AM, Exodus 3:14). The name and nature of God is shown to be connected with the verb 'to be'. God is the supreme 'being'. But what's this saying? Simply this: God is the kind of being who cannot possibly **not** be. His existence is not dependent on anything outside of himself. Rather, everything outside of him depends on him for its existence. And so, he's the kind of being without whom 'nothing' must evermore remain absolutely 'nothing.'

The idea of things spontaneously generating themselves out of nothing has been well and truly scientifically debunked. Yet, somehow – and quite irrationally – the notion lingers on that if we replace the requirement of spontaneity with indeterminate vast quantities of time, then somehow it's possible. The society which now considers itself too educated to believe in the story of the Child in the manger, can unthinkingly bring itself to believe instead in the fish in the bath-tub; that is, given enough time, a fish (or living chemicals) could develop by itself in some bath-tub (or warm pond).

Richard Lewontin, Professor of genetics, admits: "We take the side of [evolutionary] science *in spite* of the patent absurdity of some of its constructs, *in spite* of its failure to fulfill many of its extravagant promises of health and life, *in spite* of the tolerance of the scientific community for unsubstantiated just-so stories, because we have a prior commitment, a commitment to materialism ... Moreover, that materialism is absolute, for we cannot allow a Divine Foot in the door" (*The New York Review*, p. 31, 9 January 1997). Quite an admission. It will be our aim is this book to show this amounts to nothing other than the beliefs of those whom the Apostle Paul described as those who "suppress the truth in unrighteousness" (Romans 1:18). In the twenty-first century, there is absolutely no reason to be 'ashamed of the gospel' (Romans 1:17) - far from it; no more intellectually satisfying position is possible.

However, in maintaining that view, we can expect to be challenged, even as we will find it unavoidable to do other than challenge the prevailing worldview. "Always be prepared to make a defence to anyone who calls you to account for the hope that is in you" (1 Peter 3:15). That was the Apostle Peter's inspired advice geared towards helping thoughtful non-Christians. The word he uses for 'defending' or 'making a defence' is the word from which the term 'apologetics' comes. Not that Christians have to apologize for their faith, but it's our responsibility to always be ready to defend it. Nor should we think even for a moment that we can argue people into God's kingdom. Not at all. While it's necessary that we can defend our beliefs, any reasoned argument we can make will never be sufficient in itself. The power of logic cannot do what only the power of God's Spirit can. But the Spirit of God can use us – just as he used the Apostle Paul when he reasoned, explained, gave evidence and persuaded the crowds at Thessalonica (Acts 17:1-4).

But notice again with me the Apostle Peter's words. He asks his fellow-believers to be prepared to give an answer; and if we're to be prepared to give an answer to anyone who asks after the reason for the hope we have, then that must imply that our lives have already been drawing out questions from others – our lives must have already been declaring the sure hope that we have in Christ. The fact that we have such a living hope should make our lifestyle choices distinct from people around us, and that in turn should stimulate discussion. We need to be prepared for that discussion.

We've to be prepared to give an answer – literally, an 'apologetic' answer, by which we mean an answer that defends our faith. Apologetics is the term that's usually applied to the kind of pre-prepared answer we might give to questions or statements like those we'll be looking at in this book. We need to be assured that there's a solid basis for what we believe in God's Word, one which cannot be overturned. The Christian faith is a reasonable faith. God, graciously, has furnished us with evidence we can use. Another point from the Apostle Peter is that we've not to reflect back any malice coming to us from the questioner. That's not the spirit of Christ, who did not revile those who reviled him. We're to give our answer with gentleness and respect. This will glorify God, and may be used by him to bring about conviction in the heart of even a foul-mouthed accuser!

Our approach in this book will be to debunk the chapter headings which follow from the supposition (as stated in the title on the book's cover) that atheism is true. Any premise which leads logically to false conclusions is demonstrably false.

CHAPTER TWO: "ATHEISM MAKES MORE SENSE THAN CHRISTIANITY"

At Athens, the ancient centre of learning, Paul's reasoned case for Christianity caught the attention of some who belonged to various schools of philosophy. Some of them effectively wrote Paul off as a 'babbler.' The actual word they used literally described Paul as a 'seed-picker.' It seemed to picture someone gathering up seeds in order to scrape together a meal for himself, just as some desperate person today might sift through rubbish bins or garbage cans in order to find enough food to live on. Applied to Paul, they were sneeringly suggesting that here was a poorly educated person who travelled around picking up other people's ideas and feeding on their opinions before trading in them as though they were his own. They couldn't have been more wrong. There are those who give a reasoned case for Christianity today – and they get sneered at too. The sneering may raise a popular cheer, but the intellectual case for Christianity is stronger.

Consider, first, how, if atheism is true, then life is ultimately without purpose:

The Nobel prize-winning scientist Steven Weinberg, an outspoken atheist, writes: 'The more the universe seems comprehensible, the more it also seems pointless. But if there is no solace in the fruits of our research, there is at least some consolation in the research itself ... The effort to understand the universe is one of the very few things that lifts human life a little above the level of farce, and gives it some of the grace of tragedy' (from *The First Three Minutes*). Weinberg considers life as being ultimately without purpose, but he does talk about how a passion for actually doing science gives life a temporary lift above the level of farce – and he finds a crumb of comfort in that. On the other hand, a real sense of purpose is to be found in the Bible's proposition that "we [were] ... created in Christ Jesus for good works, which God prepared beforehand so that we would walk in them" (Ephesians 2:10).

Consider also, how, if atheism is true, then life is ultimately without meaning:

In an address to the American Academy for the Advancement of Science in 1991, Dr. L.D. Rue encouraged his distinguished audience to cheat on their atheistic worldview if they wanted to be happy. He recommended that they should deceive themselves into believing some kind of 'Noble Lie' which gave them and the universe some meaning. He said: 'The lesson of the past two centuries is that intellectual and moral relativism is profoundly the case.' He explained that this, when taken to extreme, results in a drive by each of us to live only for ourselves without a sense of community. To avoid the fabric of society being destroyed in this way, Dr. Rue saw only two possible solutions to overcome this logical result of atheism. One was a totalitarian state, where the wishes of individuals were suppressed by the state imposing its own values on all of society (he didn't want that). The alternative was to embrace some form of Noble Lie.

A Noble Lie 'is one that deceives us, tricks us, compels us [to go] beyond self-interest, beyond ego, beyond family, nation, [and] race.' Why call it a lie? His answer was because it tells us the universe is infused with value and because it makes a claim to universal truth – things which atheists deny. Rue adds: 'Without such lies, we cannot live.' On the other hand, Jesus Christ said: "I am the way, the truth and the life." What Dr. Rue judged to be missing is in reality to be found in Christ, and in the Noble

Truth of Christianity, when Christ's faithful followers live selflessly "for the interests of others" (Philippians 2:4).

Consider also, how, if atheism is true, then life is basically unliveable:

The German philosopher Nietsche, who died in the year 1900, made popular the saying: 'God is dead.' People at that time failed to realize - and many still do - the consequences of killing God philosophically by declaring he doesn't exist. That's why Nietsche concluded 'I have come too early. This tremendous event is still on its way' (from The Madman). But 45 years after his death, the time had come, and everyone since then should know the terrible consequences of believing there's no God. The point Nietsche anticipated was this: in a world which believes there's no God, objective right and wrong can't exist, and so all things may be permitted. When Nietsche's fellow-country-man, Hitler, put Nietsche's ideas into practice, the world soon learnt the horrors that follow when we live consistently with the idea that God is dead, and life is senseless. If God doesn't exist, then our world becomes an Auschwitz. This is man without God. It's life without sense. On the other hand, Jesus claimed: "I came that they may have life, and have it abundantly" (John 10:10).

Consider, finally, how, if atheism is true, then it's not supported by scientific explanation:

Atheistic scientists like Richard Dawkins concede that science has no 'strongly satisfying' explanation for why the universe appears to have been fine-tuned with the precise conditions ideally suited to life as we know it, but he urges his readers (*The God Delusion*, pp.157-158) 'not to give up hope' in 'some kind of multiverse theory' (the totally speculative idea that a trillion trillion parallel universes exist simply to explain the remote chance of this one being as it is). In this unpublicized section,

Dawkins appeals to his readers not to give up hope in the discovery of some new scientific theory that will one day save atheism! On the other hand: "that which is known about God is evident ... for God made it evident ... for since the creation of the world His invisible attributes ... have been clearly seen ... through what has been made ... [but] they did not honour Him as God ... but they became futile in their speculations" (Romans 1:19-21).

I think it's time to have a little bit of history. Leading the siege of Syracuse in 213BC was a Roman general Marcus Claudius Marcellus, whose nickname was "The Sword of Rome." When Marcellus brought his troops and the Roman navy up against the citadel of Syracuse, the Romans encountered frightful war machines they'd never seen before, and far more sophisticated than anything the Romans had invented. One of those war machines was especially astonishing and downright terrifying to the Roman navy: as their ships approached the cliffs outside Syracuse, the sailors looked up and saw huge jaws descending from the sky. These jaws came down, gripped a Roman ship, hoisted that ship a hundred feet or so into the air, and then the jaws released the ship and crew dashing them upon the rocks. The Romans couldn't believe what they were seeing as ropes and metal manipulated by the unheard of technical marvels of pulleys and levers, came down and gripped their ships. However, eventually, the Romans were victorious.

General Marcellus' command was that the engineer who'd developed these new weapons was to be unharmed, when and if he was found. But as a Roman soldier approached the engineer as he was sitting with other prisoners; he found him passing the time by doing mathematical equations in the sand. The man was so absorbed in calculation that he didn't notice it was a Roman soldier. Without taking his eyes off his calculations in the sand he said, "Be careful! Do not disturb my diagrams!" And the Roman soldier killed him on the spot. And thus Archimedes met his death ...

Greek by birth, born in 287BC in Syracuse to Greek parents, educated in Alexandria, Egypt, Archimedes went on to become a remarkable mathematician, an exacting engineer, a brilliant inventor, a master craftsman, a skilful builder, and something of a philosopher. It was Archimedes who, so it is claimed, after having figured out the laws of buoyancy as he was stepping into his bathtub, ran into the streets naked crying out "Eureka! (I've found it!)". Archimedes defined the principle of the lever, and is credited with inventing the compound pulley. He was one of the most brilliant men, not only of the ancient world, but of all time. You may know the words he spoke to the king of Syracuse on one occasion: "Give me a lever long enough, and a place to stand, and I will move the whole world." A little over two hundred years after Archimedes made that statement a lever was indeed found that was long enough to move the whole world. Revealed in the Gospel of the cross is the power of God to set right a topsy-turvy world. It was the message of the cross, which created the necessary leverage that continues to change the world.

Acts 17:6 reads, "These men who have turned the world upside down ..." when referring to Paul and Silas who used that Gospel lever to turn their world upside down. By the way, when the Bible speaks of turning the world upside down, it's really speaking in terms of turning the world right side up. For we live in a topsy-turvy world, a world where all around us the wicked prosper, and the righteous suffer; where sin is often exalted, and virtue mocked; a world in which it's been said that "Beggars ride on horseback while princes walk in rags." Ever since Eden, this world has been the wrong way up. And the message of Christianity is about what God has done, through the cross of Christ, to turn the world the right way up again.

CHAPTER THREE: "WE DON'T NEED GOD TO CREATE LIFE ANYMORE!"

It's a slang English expression – the saying, 'he doesn't have a leg to stand on' – but perhaps most will have heard of it. In any case, if you haven't, it means a person can't even begin to defend his or her point of view. What you may not be aware of is the fact that more or less that very same expression is found in the New Testament of the Bible – twice in fact – and both within the space of a few verses found towards the end of Romans chapter one and the beginning of chapter two.

'Apologetics' is the name given to defending Christianity; which, as we've already seen, is what we're called on to do in 1 Peter 3:15 – that is, to make a defence of the Christian hope within us. Sometimes, it seems as if we're on the back foot when doing this. The Media, often with inaccurate conclusions drawn from an all too simplistic misunderstanding of science, dismisses what it scornfully sees as our indefensible position. At times an atheistic scientist promotes a one-sided account of his or her specialist subject and so becomes the Media's favourite poster child. Even an expert scientist can be a very amateur philosopher, and straying into that territory he or she can make an impressive, but flawed, attack on Christianity.

So, the Bible calls upon Christians to make a defence of their position. But it goes even further than that: it goes on the offensive. And it does that in the section of the Bible letter which the apostle Paul wrote to the Christians who were then at Rome. Twice, very boldly, the Bible says there (Romans 1:20; 2:1) that it's those who refuse to acknowledge God who are quite literally in an indefensible position! They are said to be 'without excuse', meaning they have no defence. Of course, they would be the last people to think that! This is very far from their perception of reality while they continue to "suppress the truth" (Romans 1:18), having "exchanged the truth of God for a lie" (Romans 1:25) – for "even though they knew God" (Romans 1:21), they no longer "see fit to acknowledge God" (Romans 1:28). In place of the popular assumption that it's Christianity which doesn't have a leg to stand on, the Bible presents the opposite view that it's actually atheism which has no leg to stand on. Although in Romans chapter 1 Paul is arguing against polytheism, those arguments can equally apply in principle to today's atheism.

But, as we all know, it's one thing to make a claim, it's quite another matter to support it convincingly with compelling arguments. But Paul goes on to do exactly that. In fact, he gives four main supports. All are contained in the first three chapters of the letter which was first written to the Romans and which is preserved as the sixth book of the New Testament. The first, which is found in Romans chapter one, concerns the evidence from creation all around us. Its testimony points to the existence of the one true God whom the Bible reveals. Here's how the apostle Paul makes that point: "For [God's] invisible attributes, namely, his eternal power and divine nature, have been clearly perceived, ever since the creation of the world, in the things that have been made. So, they [that is, those who deny the true Creator God] are without excuse" (Romans 1:20).

Simply put, what Paul is saying is this: creation is evidence of a creator, as design is evidence for a designer. In particular, life is evidence for a life-giver in the shape of the living God. The extremely delicate complexity of the arrangements necessary for life on this planet are far less well explained by the assumption or belief that life is purely the result of an accidental combination of chance events. Then, again, in the words of Stephen Hawking, "The laws of science, as we know them at present, contain many fundamental numbers – [these numbers are associated with gravity, magnetism, nuclear energy, how carbon-based life works and indeed how the universe is expanding, ... Hawking continues] – the remarkable fact is that the values of these numbers seem to have been very finely adjusted to make possible the development of life." Scientists say that if any one of these numbers was different by as little as one part in a thousand, life as we know it would not seem possible.

And this is such a remarkable fact that Antony Flew, an academic philosopher who promoted atheism for most of his adult life, stated that the fine-tuned universe arguments convinced him to the point where he said: "I am very much impressed [with] the case for Christianity" (A. Flew, *'There Is a God'*). It was as if he finally accepted that he was 'without excuse' in refusing to believe in God. His last book is called *'There is a God: How the World's Most Notorious Atheist Changed His Mind.'*

Some strident atheist voices today are quite mistaken as to the true nature of faith, and seem to think it's only some kind of poor substitute for evidence. They keep demanding that we should go by empirical results – meaning opinions based on experience and observation rather than vague theory. Well then, science at its most empirical says: life comes from life; life doesn't come from non-life. The ancient Greeks had believed that small animals such as worms, mice, and maggots sprang to life automatically from the non-living matter around (such as rotting flour, a sweaty shirt, or decaying meat). This belief that living matter arose from non-living material is called 'spontaneous generation'. The idea of maggots coming spontaneously to life out of decaying meat was successfully challenged in 1668 by Italian biologist

Francesco Redi. When he covered the meat with gauze to prevent flies from laying their eggs on it, no maggots appeared in the meat. (The maggots are actually the larvae which hatch from flies' eggs.)

150 years ago, Frenchman Louis Pasteur confirmed this result, proving once and for all that spontaneous generation doesn't happen. So there's no empirical evidence for life arising without the necessity for the existence of God. There's no such thing as a simple cell. The so-called simplest bacterial cell is still a veritable factory of a hundred thousand million atoms – much more complex than anything which we humans have ever made. The gulf between this and anything non-living is as vast and absolute as anyone could care to imagine. Antony Flew, the converted atheist whose comments about the fine-tuned universe we quoted earlier, also concluded from the microscopic world of the cell that the almost unbelievable complexity of the arrangements which are needed to produce (life), [shows] that intelligence must have been involved.

But you may vaguely remember a news headline from some time ago claiming life had been artificially created in the laboratory (the work of Craig Venter). Headlines are, however, often misleading. Let's try to explain what really happened. Just as computers use a computer code made up of programmed instructions, the cells in our body use the genetic code. In other words, cells process information (in order to make proteins and other cell bits) in a similar way to computers. The living cell is like an incredibly powerful computer. What was done in that publicised lab experiment was the equivalent of making a careful copy of one version of Microsoft Windows, and turning to another computer which had previously been using a different version of Microsoft Windows and loading instead this new copy version onto it, so that when we next switch it on, that computer can now do some things it couldn't do before.

But this process doesn't involve developing a totally new brand of software; nor does it involve building computer hardware that did not exist previously. It used a software design and a computer which already existed – which means the headline about life having been created in the laboratory was very misleading. We said that cells are like computers, and most of the workings of the cell are best described, not in terms of material stuff – which we might call the hardware – but in terms of information or software. So, trying to make life by just mixing chemicals in a test tube – as in earlier laboratory experiments (e.g. Stanley Miller's) - is like soldering switches and wires in an attempt to produce Microsoft Windows. That's confusing hardware with software. Which leaves scientists (such as Paul Davies) still puzzling to this very day over how life could have arisen from non-living chemicals. The key question is, how did the hardware of non-living molecules ever manage to write its own software?

You see, understanding the chemistry as we do still doesn't help us to explain the origin of information. It's clear that the physical layout of letters on a printed page is independent of the chemical make-up of that printed page, and it's also true that the physical order of the chemical DNA letters is independent of their chemistry. But it's precisely the arrangement of letters – either on a page or in our cells – that gives meaning and holds the vital information. And so it follows that chemistry experiments can never explain life's origin. Only the existence of God can explain the origin of information, and so atheism is indefensible.

CHAPTER FOUR: "THERE'S NO SUCH THING AS RIGHT OR WRONG"

Each summer I'm involved, with many others, in running Bible camps for youngsters. The aim is to train young people to think through for themselves what the Bible teaches. Camps like this have been taking place for many decades around the world. They're still effective. They're even seen to be effective. That must be the case, because they're being copied by those who have an alternative agenda. Rival camps have in recent years been launched in the United Kingdom (e.g. CampQuest UK) – camps which are aimed at promoting a humanist or atheist philosophy. Promotional material for these camps stress they aim to encourage critical thinking and a scientific approach – all geared to helping youth reach their own conclusions.

Well, any Christian camp I've ever been involved in has also aimed to encourage critical thinking skills and personal decision-making. So what's the difference? Simply a different framework of beliefs. No evidence – certainly none about past events – speaks for itself. It has to be evaluated using critical thinking. But that thinking itself operates based on a set of background beliefs or assumptions – whether atheistic or Christian. To imply otherwise is to admit we're self-deceived. For the reality that all human reasoning takes place within a framework of beliefs has readily been acknowledged by some great men of science (e.g. Michael Polanyi FRS, 1891-1976). The whole point then becomes: which belief system is the best to reason from when explaining the evidence?

At the beginning of the letter to the Romans, the apostle Paul sets out how the Christian belief system can be easily defended. This, it has to be said, was not his primary goal, but in the space of the first three chapters of Romans, the apostle Paul uses no less than four arguments which can serve the purpose of defending the Christian faith at the most basic point of arguing for the existence of God. And the provocative claim of the Bible found twice in Romans chapters one and two is that it's really the humanists and atheists who have no defence – who are simply 'without excuse.'

So we come to the second of those four arguments, which is found in Romans chapter two, and concerns the testimony of our conscience. There, Paul writes: "For when Gentiles who do not have the Law do instinctively the things of the Law, these, not having the Law, are a law to themselves, in that they show the work of the Law written in their hearts, their conscience bearing witness and their thoughts alternately accusing or else defending them, on the day when, according to my gospel, God will judge the secrets of men through Christ Jesus" (Romans 2:14-16).

Many everyday expressions in the western world have come from the Bible in its King James Version translation. And what we've just read contains an example – when we read the words: 'a law to themselves'. Interestingly, when we hear people being accused of being a law to themselves, it seems to be generally implying that they're rebellious and out of control. But that's not how the Bible uses it here. In fact, it's the very opposite! Paul was saying that it was to the Jews that the Law was given with its Ten Commandments. These commands weren't formally given to non-Jews or Gentiles. But even so, when Gentiles end up doing, by instinct, the very things which the Law commands then they're demonstrating that the same Law has in fact been written on all our hearts. So, it's correct behaviour that becomes evidence of a hidden law – written, not on external stone tables – but actually inside us on the tables of human hearts. And notice that Paul describes it as 'the Law': it's God's Law. This Law, written on human hearts, is the basis for our conscience. This is what shows that we're moral beings.

But how is this a second evidence for God's existence? Paul has already used the wonder of creation as his first evidence back in chapter one of Romans (v.20); now in chapter two (v.15) he proceeds to a second form of evidence. Because it's here that he draws our attention to 'the moral law within'. Those last four words were quoted from Immanuel Kant, the 18th century German philosopher, who said, "Two things fill the mind with ever new and increasing admiration and awe ... the starry heavens above me and the moral law within me." These two things mentioned by Immanuel Kant capture respectively the two points we're drawing out from the Apostle Paul's first two chapters written to Christians at Rome.

So how is this 'moral law within' a second evidence for God's existence? Well, from the atheistic point of view, apart from their social consequences, there's really nothing basically wrong with many socially unacceptable things – things like when a man rapes a woman. Because without God there isn't any absolute standard of right and wrong which imposes itself on our conscience. Without God, morality becomes nothing more than a matter of personal taste or social conditioning. This is exactly the point many people have pressed on me in conversations about faith when they try to tell me that our attitude to something like rape basically only comes down to what our parents and society have taught us. You've got to then ask them where their parents got their values from ... and where their grandparents got theirs from ... and so on all the way back to the first ever humans. And at that point it's a problem. For blind forces of nature can't explain the origin of any absolute morality.

The late J.L. Mackie of Oxford University, one of the most influential atheists of our time, admitted, "If ... there ... are objective values, they make the existence of a god more probable than it would have been without them ... [there is] ... a defensible argument from morality to the existence of a god ..." Notice his words: 'a defensible argument.' On the other hand, Paul, in Romans, has just said atheists have no defence for their claim that there is no God, while proceeding to give at least four defences of Christianity in terms of assuring his readers of God's existence. So, Paul's locked horns with the atheists, and we're faced with a clear-cut choice, but it's one we can easily put to the test. On the one hand, the Word of God says objective moral values really do exist, and deep down we all know it; on the other hand, atheism says objective, absolute moral values don't exist – while admitting that if they did exist, that would give the game away.

Richard Dawkins agrees that rape is wrong, but concedes that in arriving at that view, his value judgement is every bit as arbitrary as the fact we've evolved five fingers rather than six. We quote professors Mackie and Dawkins only so as to give assurance that atheists as well as Christians agree on this as a fair test. It's fair and accurate to judge the question of God's existence based on judging the question of the existence or otherwise of objective, absolute moral values.

So then, suppose you take a group of people and ask each of them, "Do you like vegetables?" Some will say, "I like vegetables," others will say, "I don't like vegetables." And that's fine. It's a subjective thing, a matter of personal taste. But what if, instead, we were to ask, "Is it okay to torture children for fun?" You'll surely agree that we've crossed a boundary line. You wouldn't expect the same group of reasonable people whose personal tastes on vegetables varied, to show the same spread of opinion on this question, would you? But why not? Because – I submit – this is no longer a subjective matter of personal taste. We've moved on to an altogether different matter: one that's an objective matter of right and wrong.

One famous writer (C.S. Lewis) illustrates the difference by making this comparison, he said: 'The reason my idea of New York city can be truer than yours is because New York is a real place existing apart from what either of us thinks.' On the other hand, if we were trying to compare ideas about some imaginary city, then neither idea could be truer than the other because there's no basis for any comparison. Our first example about vegetables was like that, but returning to our second example of torturing children, the reason why we'd agree that one reaction is truer than the other is because a real standard of absolute morality exists apart from whatever happens to be our own personal tastes and preferences. Torturing children for fun is not a morally neutral act – it's an outrageous moral abomination. It wouldn't matter in which culture we performed the experiment. We have identified a consensus on morality which transcends culture.

Actions like rape, torture, child abuse, and so forth, are not just socially unacceptable behaviour. They're moral abominations: things which are absolutely wrong. Similarly, love, equality, generosity and self-sacrifice are really good. And the point is this: if objective values cannot exist without God, but we find that they do exist, then it logically follows that God also exists.

CHAPTER FIVE: "THE BIBLE IS JUST A BUNCH OF FAIRY STORIES"

Atheism is indefensible. How often have you heard anyone say that? Probably, not very often or not at all nowadays! But the Bible goes on the offensive in the early chapters of the Apostle Paul's letter to the Romans. Twice, very boldly, the Bible says around the end of Romans chapter one that it's those who refuse to acknowledge God who are quite literally in an indefensible position! They are said to be 'without excuse,' meaning they have no defence. Of course, they'd be the last people to think that! This is very far from their perception of reality as they 'suppress the truth' (1:18), having 'exchanged the truth of God for a lie' (1:25) – for 'even though they knew God' (1:21), they no longer 'see fit to acknowledge God' (1:28).

This exposure of such a deep-seated agenda shows that even when we're equipped with a good defence, many debates will still not be winnable. Recent outreach experience again demonstrated this. We were out on the streets of a busy shopping centre engaging passers-by in conversation about Christianity. Aware of how sceptical the mood is in Western Europe in the 21st century, we were challenging the public to demonstrate any meaning in an alternative point of view. Not a few conceded that their outlook was bleak, but they claimed to genuinely feel that there was nothing beyond. The apostle Paul was no stranger to sceptics, even in the first century. The kind of reasoning, explaining and giving of evidence (Acts 17:2,3) which he engaged in was also balanced with discernment of the predisposition of unpersuaded sceptics. But this still resulted at the end of the day in some sneering, others requesting a second hearing, while yet others ended up believing (vv.32-34). Jesus, in his testimony before Pilate, spoke of those who were 'on the side of truth' (John 18:37 NLT). They were the ones to hear his voice. Sometimes our defence will be more about honouring God than winning arguments, whenever we encounter those whom God himself has given over to a reprobate or 'depraved mind' (Romans 1:28).

But by the time Paul reaches Romans chapter 3, he's not yet done with his audience. He has already presented two important strands of evidence. He's talked about 'the starry heavens above and the moral law within.' Both point to the God who's there. But now, at the beginning of Romans chapter 3, the apostle Paul introduces "Communication" as a third supporting strand of evidence – evidence which supports the contention that God exists. Paul asks: "Then what advantage has the Jew? Or what is the benefit of circumcision? Great in every respect. First of all, that they were entrusted with the oracles of God" (Romans 3:1-2). By 'oracles', Paul is speaking about God's revelation, especially in its written form as had been entrusted to the Jewish people in terms of the writings of Moses and the other prophets as well as the writers of psalms like King David. Including now the New Testament, to which Paul himself contributed 13 letters, the completed Bible was written over a period of some 1,600 years and penned by some 40 different individuals over that time.

What's more, the Bible contains many predictions. In fact, it's been estimated that at the time of writing some 25% of the Bible was prophecy, in other words claims about the future. Now, anyone can make predictions, but having those prophecies fulfilled is something else. What's the chance, for example, of predicting in which city some future world leader is going to be born? Or the exact way in which he's going to meet his death? But this is what the Bible did – hundreds of years in advance of the events. The late Peter Stoner, Professor Emeritus of Mathematics and Astronomy at Pasadena City College, actually calculated the chance or probability of one man fulfilling the major prophecies made in advance in the Bible about the Messiah, Jesus. The estimates were worked out by twelve different classes, which amounted to some 600 university students.

Professor Stoner also encouraged other sceptics or scientists to make their own estimates to see if his conclusions were more than fair. Finally, he submitted his figures for review to a committee of the American Scientific Affiliation (Peter Stoner, *Science Speaks*, Chicago: Moody Press, 1969, p.4).

For example, concerning Micah 5:2 which says that the Messiah would be born in Bethlehem, Stoner and his students determined the average population of Bethlehem from the time of the prophet Micah right through to the present; and then they divided it by the average world population over the same period. By expressing that ratio, they calculated that the chance of one particular man being born in Bethlehem was one in 300,000 (in the same sense as the chance of getting 'heads' in any one flipping of a coin is one in two).

Then they examined not one but eight different Bible prophecies about Jesus, the Messiah. The likelihood of them all being true by chance was found to be so small that we'll have to describe it by means of an illustration. If you make a mark on one out of ten tickets, and then place all the tickets in a hat, and thoroughly stir them, and then ask a blindfolded man to draw one, his chance of getting the one ticket which you've marked is one in ten. Now suppose that instead of tickets we take silver dollar coins - and not just 10 of them – but we take a very large number of coins. Next, let's suppose we lay all these silver dollars all over the state of Texas in the US until we cover the whole of that state to a depth of two feet or in other words to a depth of about 60 centimetres. Now once again let's mark just one out of all these silver dollars and stir the whole lot of them thoroughly, all over the state. By the way, you may be interested to know that Texas is almost 3 times the size (area) of the UK. Once again, we're going to blindfold a man and tell him that he can travel as far as he wishes within Texas, but he must pick up just one silver dollar and hope that it's the right one. What chance would he have of getting the right one? [It's actually 1 chance in a 1 followed by 17 zeros]. Just the same chance - Professor Stoner worked out - that the prophets would have had of writing these eight prophecies and having them all come true in any one man, from their day to the present time, providing they wrote them in their own wisdom alone, assuming God had nothing to do with the Bible.

But, of course, there are many more than eight prophecies. In another calculation, Stoner used 48 prophecies and arrived at the estimate that the probability of 48 prophecies being fulfilled in one person is one chance in an exceedingly large number, a number which is a 1 followed by 157 zeros! Remember, for the sake of comparison, a one in a million chance is one chance in a number which is a 1 followed by only six zeros. But here we're talking about one chance in a number which is a 1 followed by – not six – but 157 zeros. So, to all intents and purposes, 48 Bible prophecies have a zero chance of being fulfilled on the basis of blind chance!

But even that's the result of considering only 48 of the Bible predictions about the coming Messiah – all of which in fact came true in Jesus of Nazareth hundreds of years later. One Bible expert (Edersheim) reckons there were actually up to 456 different prophecies available for Professor Stoner to select from had he so wished. Obviously, the chance of all this being pure coincidence is vanishingly small. There can really only be one explanation for the Bible. One preacher, R.A. Torrey, asks us to suppose that stones for a temple were brought from quarries in Rutland, Vermont, Berea, Ohio, Kasota, Minnesota, Middleton and Connecticut. Each stone was first hewn into its final shape at its own quarry before being transported to the actual temple site. Among the stones was a great variety of sizes and shapes, like cubes and cylinders. But when they were all brought together, it turned out that every stone fitted perfectly into its allotted place. What would that show? It would show, Torrey said, that at the back of all these individual quarry workers was a single architectural mastermind.

He went on to say that it's exactly like that with God's temple of truth - the Bible. How else could some 40 different human authors contribute to this one, vast project spanning some 1,600 years from start to completion? The marvellous cohesion, the wonderful consistency of the Bible, with its focus on the central picture of Christ can only mean one thing – that behind all those individual human authors there stands one divine author, who masterminded the Bible as his communication to this world.

CHAPTER SIX: "JESUS DIDN'T REALLY EXIST (AND EVEN IF HE DID, HE NEVER CLAIMED TO BE GOD!)"

If there is a God, you'd certainly expect him to communicate, wouldn't you? And as we saw in the previous chapter, the evidence is that the Bible is just such a communication from the God who's there and who gave his Son, Jesus, for us. In the early chapters of his Bible letter to Christian believers at Rome 2,000 years ago, Paul presented four indisputable evidences which point beyond the shadow of a doubt to the existence of God. But, you may ask, have they become weakened over the 2,000 years which have since run their course? Not a bit of it! In fact, they seem much more impressive today than they could ever have appeared to be all those years ago. And they're also easy to remember as the fours 'C's of Creation, Conscience, Communication and finally, Christ.

Yes, to complete our list of four Cs, we have Christ himself, bringing us to what Paul writes in Romans chapter 3: "... for all have sinned and fall short of the glory of God, being justified as a gift by His grace through the redemption which is in Christ Jesus; whom God displayed publicly as a propitiation [or sin atoning sacrifice] in His blood through faith" (Romans 3:23-25).

One very clear case of atheists not having a leg to stand on occurs in connection with what Professor Richard Dawkins says about Jesus Christ. He says: 'It is possible to make a serious case that Jesus never existed.' I put it to you that all that statement shows is that we've all got some kind of bias that goes against our better judgement (Romans 1:18b). Let me illustrate what I mean. I remember once having an old car which I'd patched up. When it came time for it to go in for its test of roadworthiness I was really hoping it would get a pass certificate. I was hoping against my better judgement, since the car probably wasn't very safe. I was biased against accepting any view of the test inspector which was in conflict with my own self-interest - and anything that was going to cost me money to have it repaired properly was against my self-interest, or so I thought. In the same way, it's just as easy for us to be biased against accepting a view of God if it seems to conflict with our own self-interest. We may not always want a God who's fair - especially if we're conscious of our own shortcomings. That's just one possible bias we might have against discovering the truth.

Having said that, let's face up to Dawkins' challenge when he says: 'it is possible to mount a serious, though not widely supported, historical case that Jesus never lived at all.' Actually, this is nonsense. Quite frankly, Dawkins should stick to science, for the actual fact of the matter is that few scholars would disagree that a man named Jesus lived roughly between 2BC and about 33AD. History documents that this man was not a myth, but a real person and the historical evidence for this is excellent. The Roman historian Tacitus, writing in about 115AD, noted Jesus' existence when recording the events surrounding Emperor Nero in July of 64AD. After the fire that destroyed much of Rome, Nero was blamed for being responsible: 'Consequently, to get rid of the report, Nero fastened the guilt and inflicted the most exquisite tortures on a class hated for their abominations, called Christians by the populace. Christus [Christ], from whom the name had its origin, suffered the extreme penalty during the reign of Tiberius at the hands of one of our procurators, Pontius Pilate ...' In fact, there's far more documentary evidence for the life of Jesus Christ than there is for Julius Caesar – and you don't hear many people disputing that Caesar was a historical character, do you?

Then there's W.H. Lecky, who wrote a history of Europe in which he stated that the impact of the three public years of Jesus' ministry had a more profound impact than all the writings of moralists and philosophers have ever had. Ah, you say, I'm happy to concede that Jesus Christ truly existed, and that he was a good man whose moral teachings have proved beneficial to many, but what if the 'Jesus of history' and the 'Jesus of faith' are two different persons? Well, it's easy to be biased, as we've shown, and it's easy to be cynical: one speaker visiting a school assembly to talk to the children about God asked for questions. One lad near the back of the hall smirked as he asked: 'You ever seen God, mister?' The speaker paused for a moment, then said: 'No, but if I'd been around 2,000 years ago, I could have!'

Former US president, Ronald Reagan, once said (and this touches on the 'Jesus of history' being the 'Jesus of faith'): 'meaning no disrespect to the religious convictions of others, I still can't help wondering how we can explain away what to me is the greatest miracle of all ... A young man whose [supposed] father is a carpenter grows up working in his father's shop. One day he puts down his tools and walks out of his father's shop. He starts preaching on street corners and in the nearby countryside, walking from place to place, preaching all the while, even though he is not an ordained minister. He does this for three years. Then he is arrested, tried and convicted. There is no court of appeal, so he is executed at age 33 along with two common thieves. Those in charge of his execution roll dice to see who gets his clothing - the only possessions he has. His family cannot afford a burial place for him so he is interred in a borrowed tomb. End of story? No, this uneducated, property-less young man who ... left no written word has, for 2000 years, had a greater effect on the world than all the rulers, kings, emperors; all the conquerors, generals and admirals, all the scholars, scientists and philosophers who have ever lived - all of them put together. How do we explain that? ... unless he really was who he said he was."

The decision we have to make concerning the identity of the historical Jesus has famously been presented like this. Jesus Christ himself claimed to be the Son of God, and so the only options for us are: that he was either a liar or a lunatic or truly Lord of all. You see, Jesus claimed to be God's Son, which if true simply means that he's, in fact, Lord. But, if it's a false claim, then Jesus cannot be considered to have been even a good man (for they don't make false claims); so, in that case, he must have been either a liar or a lunatic (depending on whether or not he knew the claim he was making was false).

We said there that Jesus Christ claimed to be God. You might object and say "Jesus never actually said the words: 'I am God'." Perhaps that's true, but imagine you're out driving one day and your car breaks down. You call George's Garage. Half an hour later a breakdown truck pulls up in front of you with George's Garage written above the cab. The mechanic's overalls and the bill you have to sign both say the same thing: George's Garage. Very soon the car's fixed, but when you arrive home someone says to you 'but did you ask the bloke – and did he say – that he was from George's Garage'? Well, no you hadn't, but everything about the man – especially in those particular circumstances - totally convinced you.

That's like the way in which Jesus effectively claimed to be God. What he did, and everything about him, speaks for itself. What he did wasn't done in a corner. The works which were his credentials were very public. People – who were not yet his followers - said at the time that no one could do the things Jesus did unless he came from God. One, who was his follower, Peter, put it like this: "Jesus of Nazareth, a Man attested by God to you by miracles, wonders, and signs which God did through Him in your midst, as you yourselves also know" (Acts 2:22). That last point is important: Peter could say to a hostile audience "as you yourselves know". Even they couldn't dispute the facts. Whereas legends like that of King Arthur were built up over centuries; Peter was talking to Christ's contemporaries.

Born a Jew, Jesus endorsed fully the commandment: "You shall worship the LORD your God, and Him only shall you serve" (Luke 4:8). But, yet, at times, for example after healing the blind man in John chapter 9, Jesus allowed people to worship him (v.38). Put these two facts together and what else can you make of them, but that Jesus was, in fact, claiming to be God? On another occasion, Jesus caused quite a stir by publicly saying to someone: "Your sins are forgiven" (Mark 2:9). The Jewish religious authorities who were within earshot were shocked and they protested; "Who can forgive sins but God alone?" Now if someone sins against my neighbour, it's not appropriate for me to grant forgiveness simply because I'm not the offended party. But the Jews knew from their book of psalms (Psalm 51:4) that all sin is ultimately against God. And so, to them, by claiming to forgive a man's past sins, Jesus was unmistakably claiming to be God.

Jesus came to make God known to us. It's because, in Jesus, God came as man, that we really can come to know God. And you could say the kind of character Jesus displayed - in even loving his enemies, for example - is all that we could ever wish God to be like. His was the most attractive human life ever, the ultimate. Faced with that – and coupled with his astounding claims - we must make a stark choice and say either he was in fact exactly who he claimed to be, or he was bad or mad because he was a deceiver. The Bible emphatically describes him as both our Saviour and our God (see Titus 2:13)!

I'd also like to quote the refreshingly frank and even eloquent tribute given thoughtfully by Napoleon Bonaparte after he'd a lot of time for reflection during a period of exile in his life. It's recorded that he said to one of his associates that he, Napoleon, had inspired multitudes with such an enthusiastic devotion that they'd have died for him. But he said to do that it'd been necessary for him to be visibly present with the electric influence of his looks, words and voice. Napoleon went on to say that Christ alone had succeeded in so raising the mind of man toward the unseen that it became insensible to the barrier of time and space. Across a chasm of 1,800 years, Jesus Christ, he said, made a demand which is beyond all others difficult to satisfy ... [Jesus] asks for the human heart. He demands it unconditionally and forthwith his demand is granted. Wonderful! In defiance of time and space, the spirit of man with all its powers and faculties becomes an annexation to the empire of Christ. All who sincerely believe experience that supernatural love towards him. Napoleon commented, this phenomenon is unaccountable, and he said it was this that showed convincingly the divinity of Jesus Christ.

And so, we remind ourselves we've been looking at the early chapters of Paul's Bible letter to Christian believers at Rome 2,000 years ago. There Paul presents four indisputable evidences which point beyond the shadow of a doubt to the existence of God. And they're easy to remember: as all beginning with the letter C. There's the evidence from Creation (Romans 1:20); the evidence from human Conscience (2:14-16); the evidence of Communication (3:1,2) as we considered the claim of the Bible to be the Word of God – a direct communication to us from the God who's there; and the best evidence of all is Christ himself (3:23-25).

CHAPTER SEVEN: "MADE IN GOD'S IMAGE? WE'RE JUST HIGHLY EVOLVED POND SCUM!"

In the United Kingdom, in December 2012, the results of the 2011 national census were published which showed that now only one in every three people profess to be 'Christian', while one in four returned an answer of 'no religion.' The actual number of those reporting 'no religion' was 14.1 million, which when compared to 8.5 million in 2001, shows a 67% increase over 10 years. Presumably, some of these people may still have some belief in God despite not aligning themselves with any particular religious organisation. However, many of them will likely be atheists and believe in some form of naturalistic evolution, which is the view that ultimately sees humans as highly evolved pond scum. That doesn't seem to be a very appealing or even a very dignified description of human beings.

But the likes of Richard Dawkins would say 'tough, too bad, for that's just the way it is.' Dawkins once said this: 'We are going to die and that makes us the lucky ones. Most people are never going to die because they're never going to be born. The potential people who could've been here in my place, but who will in fact never see the light of day outnumber the sand grains of Sahara. Certainly, those unborn ghosts include greater poets than Keats, scientists greater than Newton. We know this because the set of possible people allowed by our DNA so massively outnumbers the set of actual people. In the teeth of these stupefying odds, it is you and I in our ordinariness that are here. We privileged few who won the lottery of birth against all odds, how dare we whine at our inevitable return to that prior state from which the vast majority can never start.'

Or, perhaps you prefer the description of human beings as recycled star stuff? Astronomer Alan Dressler has written that every atom in our bodies save hydrogen was once at the centre of a star. We'll allow Neil deGrasse Tyson to explain what he finds appealing in this point of view: 'The Big Bang endowed the universe with hydrogen and helium and not much of anything else. But there are stars, and stars manufacture heavy elements from light elements. They take hydrogen in and fuse the atoms to become helium, and helium fuses to become carbon, and carbon fuses to become silicon and nitrogen, and so on. Thus, elements other than hydrogen and helium have no origin other than [in] the centres of stars. And stars not only manufacture the heavy elements, they also explode them into space. Since life itself thrives on these heavy elements, we owe our very existence to stars. The very molecules that make up your body, the atoms that construct the molecules are traceable to the crucibles that were once the centres of high mass stars that exploded their chemically enriched guts into the galaxy enriching pristine gas clouds with the chemistry of life. So, we're all connected to each other, biologically; to the earth, chemically; and to the rest of the universe, atomically.'

It seems to me that these are attempts to give some sense of awe and dignity to a hopeless and purposeless existence, but they fail to account for the origin of information. How did the chemical hardware of our cells write its own software? Reducing everything down to chemistry doesn't really get us very far, because if you take the printed page of a book, you can indeed reduce it all down to chemistry – except for the fact that it leaves totally unexplained the fact that the page communicates information through the text – and that happens by the physical ordering of the letters, something quite independent of chemical makeup. If that's true of a single page of a book – and it is, quite indisputably – how much more is it the case that life – with all its DNA information - is more than mere chemistry.

This is where I want to emphasise the revolutionary nature of the Christian message. How and why is it radical? I would say because it's the only truly coherent worldview. What do we mean by that? First, a 'worldview' is a perspective: a way of interpreting, or making sense of, the world around us. And second, every worldview – and it doesn't matter whether we're talking about atheism, pantheism or polytheism – every single worldview has to be able to answer 4 questions, and these are: Where did we come from? What's the meaning of life? How do we define right from wrong? What happens to us when we die?

These are the four most fundamental questions of life. Every thinking person asks them at some time or other in their life. You'll have noticed, of course, that they boil down to questions of origin, meaning, morality and destiny. And the point is, that in Christ, through the Gospel, we have a coherent set of answers to these four worldview questions: in terms of humans having been created in God's image, to enjoy a relationship with our Creator, who has summarized his moral standards for us most famously in the Ten Commandments, and through the cross of Christ has secured an eternally glorious future for all who believe.

And if I was to select a verse from the Bible to highlight human dignity and contrast sharply with the bleak views presented earlier belonging to those who say there's no God, then I'd choose this one from Psalm 8: It asks, "What is man ...?" and answers, "You have crowned him with glory and honor. You have made him to have dominion over the works of Your hands; you have put all things under his feet." That was God's purpose in creation.

In moving away from the failure of any philosophy which wilfully rejects God's existence – including its failure to invest our humanness with any real sense of dignity – let's now, if we may, view ourselves biblically, and we see that human dignity is something which is derived – it descends from the revealed reality that we're created equally in the image of God. While in certain cases, that image and dignity seems to be more fittingly and prominently displayed than in other cases, nevertheless, the essential dignity of our humanness is an absolute given that doesn't rise and fall within the span of individual human existence – by which I mean it's unaffected by the degree by which our biology is as yet undeveloped or later begins to malfunction.

For even humans who exist in some degree of dependence on others are essentially no less dignified - not, when we reflect on how God by becoming flesh himself in the incarnate Christ dignified even such a state through becoming dependent on human breasts and all the other normal menial duties of care on which every infant depends. In this way, prominent aspects of helplessness are seen not to diminish our essential human dignity which, as we say, is something that's God-given.

In the book *'Finding Your Way'*, Gary LaFerla tells an amazing story, pieced together from the records of the United States Naval Institute following the Second World War. The USS Astoria had engaged the Japanese during the battle for Savo Island before any other ships of the U.S. navy arrived. During the crucial night of the battle, August 8, the Astoria scored several direct hits on a Japanese vessel, but was itself badly damaged in the process. At about 0200 hours, Signalman 3rd Class Elgin Staples, was swept overboard by the blast after the Astoria's gun turret exploded. Wounded in both legs by shrapnel and in semi-shock, he was kept afloat in the sea by a narrow lifebelt.

At around 0600 hours, Staples was rescued by a passing destroyer and returned to the Astoria, whose captain was attempting to save the cruiser by beaching her. The effort failed, and Staples, still wearing the same lifebelt, found himself back in the water! It was now lunchtime. Picked up again, this time by the USS President Jackson (AP – 37), he was one of 500 survivors of the battle who were evacuated. On board the transport, Staples hugged that lifebelt with gratitude, and studied the small piece of equipment for the first time. He scrutinized every stitch of the lifebelt that had served him so well. It'd been manufactured by the Firestone Tire and Rubber Company of Akron, Ohio, and it bore a registration number.

Given home leave, Staples told his story and asked his mother, who worked for Firestone, about the purpose of the number on the belt. She replied that the company insisted on personal responsibility, and each checking inspector had their own personal number which they put on the belt when signing it off. Staples remembered everything about the lifebelt, and quoted the number. There was a moment of stunned silence in the room and then his mother spoke: "That was my personal code that I affixed to every item I was responsible for approving." Try to imagine the emotions within the hearts of mother and son. The one whose DNA he bore had also been instrumental in his rescue in the waters that had threatened his life.

If an earthly parent can provide a means of rescue without knowing when and for whom that belt would come into play, how much more can the God of all creation accomplish? His "registration number" is on you, for God, our sovereign creator, originally imprinted his image on his human creation. Then he also took upon himself the personal responsibility for our rescue. He's the one who leaves nothing to chance in bringing all the threads together in our life story. The God who designed us with a dignity – which we've defaced - has now thrown us a lifeline in Jesus Christ – will you stretch out for the purpose you were made for?

CHAPTER EIGHT: "DEATH IS THE END AND THAT'S ALL THERE IS TO IT"

Oxford professor John Lennox says he was travelling on the train to London, and there was sitting beside him a man in his late 50s who was reading what was obviously a scientific article. Lennox said: "I see you're a scientist." He said, "That's right, I'm a metallurgist. What are you?" "I'm a mathematician", Lennox replied. Lennox next took out a New Testament and started to read it and could see after a few moments the other fellow was glancing over to see what book it was that he was reading - so he made it easy for him to see what it was. And after a moment or two he said, "Excuse me, you're reading the New Testament." Lennox said, "That's right" and went on reading. And after 3 minutes he said, "I don't want to disturb you but you did say you were a mathematician - and now you're reading the New Testament. How is that possible?"

At that point Lennox asked him: "Have you got any hope?' The metallurgist went white and started to shake; and after a moment or two he said, "I guess we'll all muddle through." But Lennox didn't let him away with that. He said, "you know that's not what my question was - have you got any personal hope?" And he said, "None whatsoever." Lennox then said: "And you ask me why I'm reading the New Testament?" The New Testament of the Bible, a copy of which was handed over that day, points to a personal hope that extends beyond the grave for those who receive its message. At a time when the apostle Paul was defending Christianity, he said: "... I am on trial for the hope and resurrection of the dead!" (Acts 23:6). So, a personal hope that stretches beyond the grave is a major, defining feature of Biblical Christianity. Christianity gives hope. It teaches the totally revolutionary concept that death is not the end, but that we can have "a hope in God ... that there will be a resurrection of both the just and the unjust" (Acts 24:15).

Christianity is unique in making the bold claim that all dead people will hear the voice of God's Son and exit their tombs in bodily resurrection bound for one of two destinies. In John 5:28, Jesus says: "All who are in the tombs will hear His voice, and will come forth." Notice, Jesus plainly says that all will be bodily raised. How better could he prove the authority of his words than by his own bodily resurrection after his sacrificial death on the cross?

Professor Thomas Arnold, former chair of history at Oxford, stated, "I have been used for many years to study the histories of other times, and to examine and weigh the evidence of those who have written about them, and I know of no one fact in the history of mankind which is PROVED BY BETTER AND FULLER EVIDENCE of every sort, than the great sign which God has given us that Christ died and rose again from the dead."

As such then, it gives objective, testable, and decisive evidence for the Christian faith. As the Apostle Paul says: "if there is no resurrection of the dead, [then] not even Christ has been raised; and if Christ has not been raised, then ... your [Christian] faith also is vain" (1 Corinthians 15:14).

Christians, Jews, and most informed atheists agree that Jesus was crucified and buried. The crucial belief for Christianity is that he was also resurrected — proving he's the Son of God, and the unique way of salvation for all who truly believe in him. As Paul says, this is the critical evidence for Christianity - and what's exciting is that it's testable as an objective fact of history, and in exactly the same way that any other historical claim can be established as fact. The questions we need to ask are: 'what's the evidence?' and 'which possible explanation best fits the evidence?'

Beginning, then, with the evidence for the empty tomb, Mark tells us, Joseph of Arimathea ... a prominent member of the [Jewish ruling] Council ... gathered up courage and went in before Pilate, and asked for the body of Jesus (Mark 15:43). This was to ensure it had a proper Jewish burial. Now, this has the ring of truth to it, for if the story of Jesus' burial was a fabrication, why would anyone take the risk of naming a well-known public figure as the surprising person responsible for this action – unless it was the truth and no-one could deny it.

Then Pilate got the Roman centurion to certify the death – which is recorded in secular histories – and then personally granted the body to Joseph. So the evidence certainly points to Jesus having died and been buried, but Matthew's Gospel goes on to support the claim of resurrection by volunteering the information that the guards who had been assigned to stand watch over the tomb of Jesus ... came into the city and reported to the chief priests all that had happened. And when they had assembled with the elders and consulted together, they gave a large sum of money to the soldiers, and said, "You are to say, 'His disciples came by night and stole Him away while we were asleep'" (Matthew 28:11-13).

So, an alternative explanation – that the disciples simply stole Jesus' body – was the first to be put forward by opponents of Christianity. But I'd like you to notice this was to explain away the empty tomb. We shouldn't skim over this. That point was conceded at the time – by those hostile to Christianity – that the tomb was standing empty!

Now for the evidence of eyewitnesses. The Gospels report that women were the first eyewitnesses of the empty tomb and the risen Christ - but the testimony of women was not legally accepted in that culture then. So, it's unlikely the Gospel writers would use it if they were simply inventing a story. The apostle Paul also appealed to eyewitness evidence for Jesus' resurrection in order to show that Christianity is true. In the fifteenth chapter of his first letter to the Corinthians, he wrote: "that Christ died for our sins according to the Scriptures, and that He was buried, and that He was raised on the third day according to the Scriptures, and that He appeared to Cephas, then to the twelve. After that He appeared to more than five hundred brethren at one time, most of whom remain until now ..." (1 Corinthians 15:3-6).

Why did Paul add that last remark – about most of the eyewitnesses being still alive at that time? Again, there's a good probability that this level of detail is evidence of a genuine account. But more than that, surely it was inviting the audience to go and interrogate the eyewitnesses themselves! This goes beyond the uncontested circumstantial evidence of the empty tomb. Here was the confident presentation of positive evidence from the lips of multiple eyewitnesses who were available for cross-examination. And the only people we know of who actually questioned the early eye-witnesses, after initially refusing to believe, later changed their verdict on the evidence and went on – many of them at least – to prominent roles in the early Christian churches.

Which brings us on finally to the evidence of transformed lives. There are two outstanding examples: James the Lord's half-brother and the rabbi, Saul from Tarsus. Their U-turn from total disbelief and violent hostility is hard to explain if the resurrection never happened. Concerning the others, Mark tells us in his

Gospel (14:50) how at the first, they all forsook [Jesus], and fled. But something immensely significant must have happened to that small band of frightened and humiliated men, for less than two months later, they went back into Jerusalem to preach boldly, at the threat of death, that Jesus Christ was alive! Luke records them saying (Acts 4:20): "For we cannot but speak the things which we have seen and heard". Many of them would go on to lose their lives for sticking to their story – their version of events. I know some will say people will die for any weird thing they passionately believe to be true – but that's not what resurrection-deniers ask us to accept. If Christ did not rise from the dead, then his followers invented it all as an enormous hoax – and we're expected to accept that these early Christians died for the sake of a lie which they themselves invented. That's quite different, and not at all likely.

Now, if you're a fair-minded person, I want to set you a challenge. One sceptic (Hume) said we should only accept a miracle has taken place if to disbelieve it would require us to accept something which seems even less likely. So, take the various explanations that are offered as fitting the evidence, for example: the 'body was stolen' theory; the 'witnesses were just hallucinating' theory; the 'Jesus later revived in the cold tomb' theory; as well as the view that Jesus really did rise from the dead: and measure each of them against just these three evidences we've looked at: the empty tomb, the number of eyewitnesses and the suddenly emboldened Christians who started Christianity. And ask yourself which of these explanations explains more of the evidence more convincingly than any other?

I'll conclude by telling you about a person who did just that. Dr. Greenleaf, the Royal Professor of Law at Harvard University, and reputedly one of the greatest legal minds that ever lived, believed the resurrection of Jesus Christ to be a hoax. But after thoroughly examining the evidence for the resurrection, Dr. Greenleaf came to the exact opposite conclusion! He even wrote a book entitled *An Examination of the Testimony of the Four Evangelists by the Rules of Evidence Administered in the Courts of Justice*. In it, he emphatically stated: 'it was IMPOSSIBLE that the apostles could have persisted in affirming the truths they had narrated, had not JESUS CHRIST ACTUALLY RISEN FROM THE DEAD' (p.29). Greenleaf concluded on the basis of the quality of legal evidence that the resurrection of Jesus Christ was the best supported event in all of history!

Remember the apostle Paul said in 1 Corinthians 15:14, "and if Christ has not been raised, then our preaching is vain, your faith also is vain". The opposite is true also: if Christ has been raised, then atheism is totally wrong!

CHAPTER NINE: "DESIGNED? THE UNIVERSE IS JUST A GIANT COSMIC ACCIDENT!"

The Bible famously begins by saying, 'In the beginning God created the heavens and the earth' (Genesis 1:1), and Christianity affirms that God brought the universe into being from nothing, creating it very precisely to support life (see John 1; Colossians 1; Hebrews 1; 11). And science most definitely affirms that this universe is quite ideally designed to support carbon-based human life. Astronomer Sir Fred Hoyle – he who invented the term 'the Big Bang' to describe the popular scientific view of how the universe began - admitted it was as likely to obtain a single protein by chance as it was for a solar system full of blind men standing shoulder to shoulder all to solve the Rubik's Cube puzzle simultaneously. And as if that wasn't enough, he added that the simplest cell arising all by chance was as likely as 'a tornado sweeping through a junk-yard ... [and] assembl[ing] a Boeing 747 from the materials therein.'

Well, and as we most likely know, some of science's best-established and most widely applicable laws point to this universe having a beginning. And one Nobel prize-winning researcher (Penzias) says that his research (into cosmology) has caused him to see "evidence of a plan of divine creation." In fact, this is exactly what he's on record as saying: "the best data we have are exactly what I would have predicted, had I had nothing to go on but the five books of Moses, the Psalms, [and] the Bible as a whole" (Browne, 1978). In other words, he's saying that the scientific data and the Bible agree on the fact that the universe had a beginning – at least that's the view of this Nobel prize-winning research scientist.

You may now be asking, 'so what's radically different about Christianity's message then? After all, it seems like science and the Bible agree on the universe having a beginning, and being wonderfully suited to supporting life.' The difference, of course, is all about 'Why?' Why is it that it's like this? Why should our universe have had a beginning, and be precisely right for life? The Discovery Channel TV program called '*How the Universe Works*', in one of its episodes entitled 'Big Bang', features commentaries by Professor Lawrence Krauss, and tells us: "Everything in the universe is made from matter created in the first moments of the Big Bang." The program then asks: "How did nothing become something?" Krauss answers: "The laws of physics allow it to happen." Then we're told: "At the instant of creation all the laws of physics began to take shape." But how can the laws of physics allow nothing to become something when these laws we're told were still taking shape then?

There is only one way of getting something from nothing (ex nihilo), and that is by an act of creation by a Creator - in fact, by the Almighty Creator God of the Bible. We occasionally hear the comment today that there's such a thing as matter being created out of a so-called 'quantum fluctuation' – this is described as being how, starting from nothing, we got equal amounts of particles and antiparticles – in a way that's just like how 'zero becomes $+1$ and -1' – two numbers whose sum together is zero. And this is often used to 'explain' how the universe popped into existence. But for this explanation to work, it would require the pre-existence of the laws of quantum physics - which is hardly 'nothing', I'm sure you'll agree.

Whenever something is being created, there's simply got to be something doing the creating. There really is no way round that.

To say something, even the universe, simply created itself is nonsense because it would first have to exist in order to create itself! Anything which has a beginning to its existence must have a cause. That seems an obviously true statement to make, but let's make sure - let's test it by running it past a famous sceptic. David Hume (1711 – 1776) was a Scottish philosopher, historian and above all, a noted sceptic. Hume wrote, "I never asserted so absurd a proposition as that something could arise without a cause" (David Hume, in J.Y.T. Greig, ed., *The Letters of David Hume*, 2 vols. (New York: Garland, 1983), 1:187.)

So, where have we got to? We've reviewed how a Nobel-prizewinning scientist has confirmed the general opinion in modern science which is that this universe had a beginning. And, added to that, we've heard how a leading sceptic has conceded that nothing can begin to exist without a cause. Taken together, both of these statements mean that the universe must have had a cause. And yet, atheism tries to tell us that the universe just happened, all by chance. And what's more, scientists have discovered that there are famously six numbers that make the equations which describe our universe work – and the stunning thing is if even a single one of them was just very slightly different then we wouldn't be here! In the words of famous scientist, Stephen Hawking, "The laws of science, as we know them at present, contain many fundamental numbers – the remarkable fact is that the values of these numbers seem to have been very finely adjusted to make possible the development of life."

Scientists who don't believe in God – unlike those who do - struggle to explain scientifically how chance, a pure fluke occurrence, could be so precise in its result. Take, for example, Richard Dawkins who's forced to concede that science has – and I quote – no 'strongly satisfying' explanation on that precise point, but urges his readers in his best-selling book, '*The God*

Delusion' (pp.157,158), 'not to give up hope' in 'some kind of multiverse theory'- which is the idea that the so-called 'Big Bang', which he believes started it all off, did so in such a way as to produce infinitely many 'pocket' universes of which our universe is but one.

This part of his book hasn't received a lot of attention, but it's actually in print that this strident voice of atheism appeals to his readers not to give up hope in the discovery of some new scientific theory that will one day save atheism! Isn't there a hint of desperation there? But through the media, the impression is still usually given that science has somehow disproved God. But how does this weird idea help Dawkins anyway? Well, it's a notion that builds on the idea that it's rare to throw 3 sixes in a row with a single die, but if instead you have enough people - 216 to be precise − and they're all throwing dice then you would in fact expect to find someone among them who does actually get 3 sixes in a row. Arguing like that, they say that if there are a trillion trillion parallel universes, you'd expect there to be one − and it turns out to be ours - which is finely-tuned in exactly the way ours is. That's really the best Dawkins' science can do as a way of explaining how we're here at all as we are.

The choice we're faced with, then, is a blind faith in a trillion trillion other universes or rational faith in a single creator God − but notice one way or the other, it's down to faith. But I'd like to ask you which kind of faith is the most reasonable? One which believes that information and powers of scientific reasoning have their source in the mind of a super-intelligent creator God; or, a faith that believes that our ability to reason arose out of random mindless processes − but is somehow still to be trusted!

As we've heard, those who sustain their atheistic belief in the 'mere appearance' of design put forward the idea - totally without evidence - that myriads of so-called parallel universes exist. What they're doing is literally trying to load the dice in their favour. But it remains the case that the extremely delicate complexity of the arrangements necessary for life on this planet are far less well explained by the assumption - or belief - that life is purely the result of an accidental combination of chance events.

What we've shared so far is all summed up in the public address which the Apostle Paul's delivered in Athens: "The God who made the world and everything in it ... made from one man every nation of mankind to live on all the face of the earth, having determined allotted periods and the boundaries of their dwelling place, that they should seek God, in the hope that they might feel their way toward him and find him. Yet he is actually not far from each one of us ...The times of ignorance God overlooked, but now he commands all people everywhere to repent, because he has fixed a day on which he will judge the world in righteousness by a man whom he has appointed; and of this he has given assurance to all by raising him from the dead" (Acts 17:27-31).

God says "come let us reason together" in Isaiah 1:18 and Jesus Christ, his Son, says "Come to me."

CHAPTER TEN: "WE JUST HAVE TO ADMIT THAT THERE'S NO REAL PURPOSE TO LIFE"

Scientific spokesman Stephen Jay Gould, lately of Harvard University, once had this to say about human origins: "We are here because one odd group of fishes had a peculiar fin anatomy that could transform into legs for terrestrial creatures; because comets struck the earth and wiped out dinosaurs, thereby giving mammals a chance not otherwise available (so thank your lucky stars in a literal sense); because the earth never froze entirely during an ice age; because a small and tenuous species, arising in Africa a quarter of a million years ago, has managed, so far, to survive by hook and by crook. We may yearn for a 'higher' answer – but none exists. This explanation, though superficially troubling ... is ultimately ... exhilarating."

How, may I ask, is that exhilarating? I'd like to come back to that later, but let's start with Stephen Jay Gould's belief that there's no higher answer – no supernatural reason – for our existence. Many are inclined to believe that (these are the words of a scientist after all), but it's worth bearing in mind that he's really talking about history here, and not about science. The view he expresses is much more a view about a version of history than it is about science. When he makes these points about what he says happened in the distant past which cannot be proven, he's of course talking about history. They are claims about what may have happened and they cannot be proved. His rejection of the Bible's revealed history is on philosophical grounds, not on scientific ones. He's presenting a particular (and very prevalent) interpretation of the evidence; but he's not presenting us with facts. Scientific facts by themselves don't argue against the Bible; but the view – the inference drawn from evidence – like the one that says nature is all there is, certainly is a worldview that conflicts with the Bible. For the Bible reveals that there's a God who is our creator. The view that sees nothing beyond nature implies that the universe itself must somehow have made us.

These are simply two alternative explanations. All explanations need to end or, if you like, need to begin, somewhere – either in the creator God of the Bible or in elementary particles. To believe that we're all just recycled star stuff is just as much a step of faith as believing 'In the beginning, God ...' For it's as easy to interpret scientific evidence in a way that's consistent with the Bible as it is to interpret the evidence in a way that opposes the Bible. It's not the evidence that gets in the way, it's the philosophical baggage surrounding it and through which we tend to view the evidence.

Now coming back to the exhilaration Stephen Jay Gould's found in believing there's no higher power, I have to confess I'm at a complete loss to understand how this view of life, the universe and everything can possibly be considered exhilarating. How is it exhilarating to think of yourself as highly developed pond scum? "The fool has said in his heart 'there is no God,'" the Bible says, and later adds some "professing [themselves] to be wise ... became fools" (Psalm 14:1; Romans 1:22). I guess this is what Malcolm Muggeridge had in mind when he said 'we've educated ourselves into imbecility.'

A cosmic accident, recycled star stuff, evolved pond scum - can anyone who believes this is all we are honestly believe that there's a real purpose to life? At most, a very limited one, I suggest. I'm reminded of some words which were spoken at the memorial service of a highly respected faculty member at an

American university: "Let us take a few minutes to reflect on the life of our friend and colleague before the winds of time cover over his footprints in the sand." Just footprints in the sand, with no lasting purpose or meaning. How sad! It seems to me that if you believe we're here by accident, then that's about as good as it gets. Yes, many seem to see a purpose and meaning in life in terms of enjoying relationships, doing satisfying work and launching their children into successful careers. That's fine as far as it goes, but it falls far short of having a personal hope beyond this life, and far short of a sense of ultimate purpose in life.

In his novel '*The Time Machine*', English writer H.G. Wells imagines a time traveller who journeys into the distant future to see what lies ahead for the human race. All he finds is a bit of moss on a dead earth orbiting a gigantic red, dying sun. The only sounds are the rush of the wind and the gentle ripple of the sea. 'Beyond these lifeless sounds,' writes Wells, 'the world was silent. Silent? It would be hard to convey the stillness of it. All the sounds of man, the bleating of sheep, the cries of birds, the hum of insects, the stir that makes the background of our lives – all that was over.' And so, Wells' imaginary time-traveller returned. But returned to what? To an earlier point on the same purposeless journey to oblivion. While this is science fiction, it does describe well the reality of a universe without God, without hope and without purpose. If we're all alone in the universe, having evolved from pond scum then this is where we're headed: to an ever more silent, cold and dead universe.

Wasn't this the same point the wise man in the Bible was making when he said: "For the fate of the sons of men and the fate of beasts is the same. As one dies so dies the other; indeed, they all have the same breath and there is no advantage for man over beast, for all is vanity. All go to the same place. All came from the dust and all return to the dust" (Ecclesiastes 3:19-20).

If there's no God, we're ultimately no better off than the animals. One outspoken atheist, Steven Weinberg, the Nobel prize-winning scientist, says: 'It is very hard to realize that this all is just a tiny part of an overwhelmingly hostile universe. It is even harder to realize that this present universe has evolved from an unspeakably unfamiliar early condition, and faces a future extinction of endless cold or intolerable heat. The more the universe seems comprehensible, the more it also seems pointless. But if there is no solace in the fruits of our research, there is at least some consolation in the research itself. Men and women are not content to comfort themselves with tales of gods and giants, or to confine their thoughts to the daily affairs of life; they also build telescopes and satellites ... and sit at their desks for endless hours working out the meaning of the data they gather. The effort to understand the universe is one of the very few things that lifts human life a little above the level of farce, and gives it some of the grace of tragedy' (from 'The First Three Minutes').

Weinberg considers a life devoted to Godless science as being ultimately without purpose. But he does talk about how a passion for actually doing science gives life a temporary lift above the level of farce – and he finds some comfort in that. But at least Weinberg is much more realistic than Stephen Jay Gould. The journey from an accidental beginning to a futile extinction is much more consistent with tragedy than exhilaration.

"All is futility," the Bible preacher said (Ecclesiastes 1:2). It certainly is – if life is no more than a jumble of random events, full of inequalities and injustices which are never going to be set right. But God has set eternity within our hearts, the Bible says (Ecclesiastes 3:11). That's basically why we all find it hard to settle for a pointless universe and the absurdity of this life – because doing that ignores the broader, eternal, perspective which we know deep down in our hearts is the right one. The writer of that ancient poetic Bible book had also wrestled with ultimate questions, looking for ultimate answers, and had confirmed from experience that there really is so much more than the narrow view which sees only that which is 'under the sun' (Ecclesiastes 1:3). Having debated it all in his mind – it seems that when we read his book, Ecclesiastes, we're reading his thoughts as he debates within himself between the narrow 'nature only' view and the broader 'God exists' view. In the end, his mind, the wisest the world has known, drew the God-fearing conclusion (Ecclesiastes 12:13). I pray you will too.

CHAPTER ELEVEN: "A REAL GOD WOULDN'T LET THE INNOCENT SUFFER"

I'm reminded of a time when Malcolm Muggeridge, the British journalist and author, had been speaking at All Soul's Church in London, UK. There followed a question and answer time in which the speaker was often called upon to defend his conversion to Christianity. After what had been described as the last question was dealt with, Muggeridge noticed a young boy in a wheelchair trying to say something. He said he would wait and take his question. The boy struggled but no words came out. 'Take your time,' Muggeridge said reassuringly. 'I want to hear what you have to ask ... I'll not leave until I hear it.'

Finally, after a real struggle, one often punctuated with agonizing contortions, the boy blurted out, 'You say there's a God who loves us.' Muggeridge agreed. 'Then - why me?' Silence filled the room. The boy was silent. The audience was silent. Muggeridge was silent. Then he asked, 'If you were able-bodied (fit), would you have come to hear me tonight?' The boy shook his head. Again, Muggeridge was silent. Then he added: 'God has asked a hard thing of you, but remember he asked something even harder of Jesus Christ. He died for you. Maybe this was His way of making sure you'd hear of His love and come to put your faith in Him.' In the answer that Muggeridge gave with empathy on that occasion, there are hints of an overall biblical framework which is available for us to use as we communicate the Christian Gospel to hurting people. If shared sensitively, it can help people to at least begin to put suffering in the broader context of God's dealings with a broken world. And what then is that Bible framework? It's one which would see suffering as a consequence of the separation that exists between God and man. And that this separation has been caused by sin. So, we can't blame God for human suffering.

The Bible tells us that God created the world in love and that he loves us individually. But if God is good, and on the side of good, why do terrible things happen – like in the mass shootings in Aurora and Connecticut back in 2012, to quote two of many possible examples? What's gone wrong? Well, the Bible's answer is that we did. The *London Times* leader column said the day after a massacre at an Infant school in Dunblane, Scotland (13 March 1996): 'Christ was born among innocent slaughter and died on the Cross to pay the cost of our terrible freedom - a freedom by which we can do the greatest good or the greatest evil'.

The Bible makes it clear that God created us with free will ... but then we chose to disobey God and do our own thing. That broke our relationship with our loving Creator. It's this separation between God and ourselves that's the cause of all the suffering that's in the world - and which will finally result in eternal separation from God unless we each personally obey the message of Christianity. For only God has the answer to this problem. And Jesus Christ is God's answer. When Jesus died on the cross, he took on himself the consequence of our disobedience. His death made a way between us and God again. By rising from the dead Jesus conquered the power of death for ever. Now God requires that we each personally repent and receive Jesus, his Son, as our Saviour.

What's more, it's clear that God's concerned about our pain - to the extent that in the person of his son, he came as a man, Jesus Christ, and 'joined us in suffering'. That was the expression used by a Church of Scotland minister when interviewed by a BBC

News reporter on December 21, 1988, when Pan Am Flight 103 exploded in the sky over the Scottish town of Lockerbie. "It was like meteors falling from the sky," one resident there said. Others told how pieces of plane as well as pieces of bodies began landing in fields, in backyards, on fences, and on rooftops. Fuel from the plane was already on fire before it hit the ground; some of it landed on houses, making the houses explode. Twenty-one houses were destroyed with 11 occupants killed. The total death toll was 270, including those on the plane. The reporter savagely turned on the minister and spat out the question: 'where is your God now?' To which the calm reply was: 'God has joined us in suffering - in the person of his son, he came as a man, Jesus Christ, and joined us in suffering.'

Beyond that, Christ's sacrificial death on the cross for our sins laid the basis for bringing all suffering to an end, but the time for that hasn't arrived yet. And until it does arrive, God uses suffering to work out his higher purposes in our lives - in a way that's not very different from how a surgical procedure involves pain but is directed towards a positive outcome for us. Perhaps that's where the Christian Gospel's perspective on suffering is at its most radical. First of all, God himself, the supreme being, has joined us in suffering. And second, before eliminating it entirely from human experience, he uses it to mature and refine Christian character (Romans 5:3-4; 1 Peter 1:6,7). Becoming a Christian doesn't guarantee freedom from physical suffering on earth while we wait for Jesus to come again and take believers away from suffering to be forever with him. The Bible teaches that God treats as a Father those who are his children by faith and this can also involve suffering for corrective purposes – just as happens in an ordinary human family.

In the town of Baguio, located north of Manila in the mountains of the Philippines, there are a number of gold mines to be found. Small cars on tracks are loaded with rock from within the mountain and emerge from an opening in the hillside. The rock is then crushed, pulverized, and submitted to various chemicals. By this process, minute particles of gold are separated from the useless shale and then submitted to fierce fires in the refining furnace. Later, the molten shining gold is poured into bricks worth tens of thousands of dollars each. Suppose that those stones in the mountains could speak and ask: 'Why do I have to be removed from my place in the hills to be pounded and pulverized, attacked by biting chemicals, and submitted to furnaces?' A reply might be: 'What use are you buried there beneath the tons of useless debris? You have within you something that's valuable, useful and beautiful. Only through this apparently destructive process can you be separated from the impurities that keep you from the usefulness, beauty and purity that might be yours.' And so, perhaps, we begin to glimpse how God – who's not the author of suffering – can still use it to shape our lives and refine our characters for his glory and the benefit of others.

In sharing the Gospel, we learn to expect the fact that events like the attack on the Twin Towers on September 11, 2001 in New York will be raised as an objection to the very existence of God. In responding to events like this, someone spoke for many when he said: 'I want to sue [God] for negligence, for being asleep at the wheel of the universe.' But we betray our instinctive morality when we react to things that happen by labelling them 'good' or 'evil'. Can words like 'good' or 'evil' really have meaning if we don't believe in God? Richard Dawkins would say 'no'. Since he doesn't believe in God, he also flatly says there's 'no evil and no good'. At least he's being consistent.

But suppose you were to accept there's no God – and so basically no 'good' or 'evil' - can we then accept that September

11 is just a morally meaningless event in a meaningless world? If we feel we can't go that far, then we're forced to draw the conclusion that a consistent atheist doesn't appear to have any answers after all – and no basis for even asking the questions about the morality of such atrocities. The more you think about it, the more the existence of evil in our world points us towards the existence of God - and not away from it. Why? Because unless we refuse to label atrocities as 'evil', we're still faced with the reality of God. Suffering remains a tragic experience, the Christian perspective is not an easy one, but the atheist alternative is simply unrealistic.

Basically, what's the relevance of Christianity to the atrocities of this groaning world? Edward Shillito, while viewing the destruction of the Great War, helpfully wrote: 'to our wounds only God's wounds can speak'. Yes, there's pain and suffering at the heart of the Christian message, but it's not only human pain: it's the pain of God. After all we've said, a question mark remains over human suffering, but we do need to put it in the context of the cross of Christ – which is the mark of divine suffering. We may have to wait for justice and peace in the world, but we can know God's forgiveness for our sins on a personal level and be at peace with him right now. For God has joined us in suffering to give us the offer of ultimately being with him in a pain-free future: "He will wipe every tear from their eyes. There will be no more death or mourning or crying or pain, for the old order of things has passed away" (Revelation 21:4).

It's been said that suffering is not a question requiring an answer; nor is it a problem requiring a solution; but rather a mystery requiring a Presence. And that Presence is one which only the world-turning Christian Gospel can furnish for us.

CHAPTER TWELVE: "THE CHRISTIAN EXPERIENCE IS ONLY PSYCHOLOGICAL"

Suppose someone wanders into the room where you are right now, and he has a fried egg dangling over his left ear. That would be weird enough, but then he claims he's getting joy, peace, satisfaction and purpose in life from this fried egg. You may think he's a crackpot, but how do you argue against what he claims he's experiencing? This may seem like a rather silly example, so I will explain. Have you ever had people treat your Christian experience in much the same way as you might react to the man we've imagined? Perhaps they try to tell you that it's all psychology when you testify to them of the joy, peace, satisfaction and sense of purpose in life which you've discovered in Jesus Christ. People say it's just a crutch for those who can't cope! Or else they suggest that Christian beliefs are mere wish fulfilment. All the imagined benefits are really only down to positive thinking, they say! How do we respond?

Well, it may help us to think back to the fried egg chap who claims he's getting joy, peace, satisfaction and purpose in life from the egg. What can you do? You can investigate his experience. How? It would be fair to make enquiries to see if anyone else has found the same benefits from this strange use of a fried egg. Then you could also make an examination of what objective facts this experience is related to. Perhaps that then helps us see the kind of evidence we need to provide for those who are sceptical of Christian experience in this way. Of course we find that, for 2,000 years, millions of people from all over the world have been making the same claims that they are experiencing forgiveness of sins and peace with God through their Christian faith. But could this be the result of some kind of pre-conditioning? If the Christian experience is to be claimed to be purely psychological, then we might expect there to be some recognizable type of person who is disposed to become a Christian.

However, when we investigate the facts, we find that converts come from every imaginable background. Let me share just a couple of examples with you. One is recent and the other dates back to the very beginnings of Christianity. We begin with a sceptic's view. British journalist Mark Tully had been revisiting the scene of Jesus' life to interview people for a BBC TV series on Jesus. He ended with his own view in which he said: "[Jesus] taught in strange riddles. He didn't convince his fellow Jews and he didn't overthrow Rome. From that failure I have come to what, for me, is the most important conclusion of all. That the hardest ... article of Christian faith, the resurrection, must have happened. If there had been no miracle after Jesus' death, there would have been no grounds for faith ... No resurrection ... no church."

I'm not sure if Mark Tully would actually claim to be a Christian, but he's definitely professing that he believes the central event of Christianity to be true: Jesus Christ did rise from the dead. I share this with you because I feel it's a clear example of a case where there was no obvious pre-conditioning to such a faith. We tend to think of journalists as hard-nosed, relentless in their pursuit of the facts. If anything, by his own admission, Mark Tully was disposed against believing when he started out on his research.

My other example is an extreme one – the conversion of Saul of Tarsus. We join the story as we find it in the Bible book of Acts, chapter 9, with Saul, the deeply taught and highly trained Jewish scholar, who detested the very name of Jesus Christ.

Approaching Damascus with his escort, he had a letter in his possession that gave him authority to hunt down any Christians he could lay hands on and bring them back to Jerusalem. It fired him with a sense of purpose. He was nearly there. It was now noon, with the sun at its brightest. Suddenly, a light shone from heaven – a light brighter than the sun. Stunned, Saul and his party fell to the ground. He was next aware of a voice of authority speaking to him by name. "Saul, Saul why are you persecuting Me?" "Who are you, lord?" he replied. The response to this enquiry utterly devastated Saul, for the voice came again, "I am Jesus whom you are persecuting." It was the name he hated, and in the vision he saw the one he had taken to be nothing but a blasphemer. How wrong can you be! After encountering Christ personally, the rest is history, as they say – all about how his life changed. He went from Saul the arch-persecutor of the early Christians, and self-confessed chief of sinners, to Paul the Christian apostle and fearless preacher, who himself suffered so much for the sake of the person he once persecuted.

We mentioned earlier how the sceptic often talks of religious experiences or conversions as arising from subtle pre-conditioning in early life. With Saul, however, there was absolutely no such pre-conditioning to accept Jesus as the Christ. Rather, the opposite; his background was one of hatred of the name of Jesus. In many respects he was different to many of the other disciples. Whereas in psychological experiments, the psychologist often attempts to keep all of the factors constant except one, in his search for explanations of modes of human behaviour; when we investigate the lives of those who become Christians, we find that there are no common threads.

We could bring the examples right up to date with modern stories of dramatic conversions featuring those whom we might have thought to be the least likely material for Christian disciples

– the likes of General Manuel Norriega, converted and baptized in a state penitentiary, and many more, including top sports stars and others from the filthy slums and barrios of developing nations. So different from relatively rich, western, well-educated church-going types who, after years of following traditional religious service, discover the Biblical truth of the need to be born again. Some of those who come to Christ, already in the eyes of the world, appear to have everything, while some are sunk in grinding poverty. Some are Ivy League graduates; others are capable only of a very simple faith. There really are no common factors.

The essence of the Christian gospel is an inward change – the new birth. It's this inward reality that's demonstrated outwardly in the dramatically changed lives of so many who become Christians. Try as he might, the psychologist cannot explain this mode of behaviour in human terms. There are no constant factors in the backgrounds of those who come to Christ. For, as in the time of Jesus' ministry, so also today, people from religious backgrounds, and others from no religious background; even thieves, gang-leaders and murderers have found new life in Jesus Christ by simple faith in Him. So there is no single type of people who become Christians.

There are those who dismiss Christianity as wishful thinking – some sort of desperate response to a felt need within themselves – or see it as merely being a crutch in life. One person I was recently talking with on the west coast of Canada was trying to argue the case that 'religion is simply not objective'. He thought of it as a purely subjective experience. When people use that argument against Christianity, they all overlook just one thing – the objective fact of Jesus Christ, from which the individual experience of every Christian derives. Underlying the faith there are the facts which lead to faith. The case for

Christianity rests on two main historic facts, set out by the Apostle Paul at the beginning of First Corinthians 15: "I make known to you ... the gospel ... that Christ died for our sins according to the Scriptures, and that He was buried, and that He was raised on the third day according to the Scriptures, and that He appeared to Cephas, then to the twelve. After that He appeared to more than five hundred brethren at one time."

There we have the fact of Christ's death, as evidenced by his burial; and the fact of his resurrection, as evidenced by his appearances. And to this testimony of the Bible, we add supporting evidence from other historical records outside the Bible. Cornelius Tacitus (55-120AD), 'the greatest historian' of ancient Rome wrote: 'Consequently, to get rid of the report, Nero fastened the guilt and inflicted the most exquisite tortures on a class hated for their abominations, called Christians by the populace. Christus, from whom the name had its origin, suffered the extreme penalty during the reign of Tiberius at the hands of one of our procurators, Pontius Pilatus, and a most mischievous superstition, thus checked for the moment, again broke out not only in Judaea, the first source of the evil, but even in Rome.'

So much for testifying to Jesus' death as an objective reality, for the case of his resurrection we turn to a legal verdict. Lord Darling, former Lord Chief Justice of England has written: 'There exists such overwhelming evidence, positive and negative, factual and circumstantial, that no intelligent jury in the world could fail to bring in the verdict that the resurrection story is true.' That's about as objective as it gets – and this, from a man totally experienced in sifting and evaluating evidence to find the real truth among all the fabrications. These are the facts on which the Christian bases his or her belief that God has entered human history in the person of Jesus Christ. He, the Son of God, came down into manhood for the very purpose of allowing himself to be crucified. And there, as the representative man, he bore our sins in his own body on the tree as God punished him there for us. He arose the third day and will yet be the Judge of all. In order for us to escape God's wrath, he commands us to repent of our sin and believe on the Lord Jesus.

The reality of the Christian gospel can be further seen to be demonstrated in the preparedness of many believers to suffer and even die because of their unshakeable conviction of its absolute trustworthiness. In this world of escapism, we actually need to turn to the Bible to find reality!

CHAPTER THIRTEEN: "THOSE SO-CALLED MIRACLES ARE SIMPLY IMPOSSIBLE"

I'd like to begin this chapter with a little illustration which is especially for those who want to rule out anything which is inexplicable in terms of our understanding of natural law: A man one day puts £20 British pounds in his bedside drawer. The next day he puts another £20 pounds into the same drawer. Then on the third day he counts the money in the drawer and finds it amounts to only £15! How can that be? How is it possible that the laws of arithmetic have been broken? Ah, you say, they've not. The laws of arithmetic have not been broken, but it seems as if the laws of England have been broken - by some thief breaking in and stealing some of the money he'd deposited there!

We will come back to this illustration at the end of the chapter, but many people prefer to accept that there must be some natural explanations for Christ's miracles. They say that it simply isn't rational to believe that Jesus literally walked on water, fed over 5,000 people with just 5 loaves and 2 fish, turned water into wine, and so on. Let's take just one of the miracles: a beggar whose blindness Jesus cured in John 9. After testifying that he was the light of the world, Jesus spat on the ground, made clay of the spittle, anointed the man's eyes and sent him to wash in the pool of Siloam. The man went away believing, and returned seeing. It was yet another wonderful miracle performed amongst countless others by the Lord Jesus Christ while here on earth. But did everyone rejoice at the power of God? Sadly, no. Even in those days there were those who refused to accept the evidence that confronted them.

Take the neighbours of the previously blind man, for example. They quickly divided into two groups. There was the group who recognized and were prepared to acknowledge in this jubilant individual the one-time beggar. The other group poured scorn on this idea. "Oh," they said, "It's certainly someone like him, but it isn't him. It can't possibly be him - just an uncanny, resemblance. It's a case of mistaken identity." One group was prepared to accept that the supernatural – an event outside normal human experience – had taken place. The other group frankly dismissed the supernatural and concluded that there just had to be a natural explanation.

As we've said, the same trends are still found. Lots of people prefer to accept that there must be some natural explanation for Christ's miracles. In the modern world, in the scientific age, some would say it's illogical to still insist on miracles. Let's pause and consider for a moment the question which the curious crowd asked the miraculously healed beggar: "What do you think of the man whom you claim opened your eyes?" That's the central issue, isn't it? Just who is Jesus? When people question the possibility of the miracles of Jesus, what they're essentially taking issue with is Jesus' claim to be the Son of God. For it's clearly not illogical, but reasonable – and indeed inevitable – to accept, without any reservation whatever, all the miracles of Jesus if we accept that he's the Son of God. The Bible teaches that this is the most important question we face in our lives; our eternal destiny depends on our decision. Do you believe Jesus Christ is the Son of God? Some people say without thinking, "Oh, I accept that Jesus Christ was a good man, but nothing more than that." But the problem is that Jesus himself claimed to be more than that. In fact, he claimed to be the co-equal, co-eternal Son of the living God who created all things.

Now, few today, if any, would dispute that Jesus Christ was a historical figure. An awareness of what ancient historians have written has put that fact beyond dispute – at least for those who take the time to acquaint themselves with the facts. I mean historians with no connection to Christianity. Jewish historians like Josephus and Roman historians like Cornelius Tacitus. The fact they didn't write from a particularly sympathetic view only helps to strengthen the case that Jesus Christ was definitely not some legendary figure. But who was he? It's clear who he claimed to be. As the Jewish religious leaders who were jealous of him, tried to build their case against him, they asked if he was the Christ, the Son of the Blessed (Mark 14:61,62). Jesus affirmed that he was. There was no secret about this. In fact, some time before, the Jews had picked up stones to stone him for what they considered to be blasphemy. Jesus had called God his father, and the Jews understood that he was making himself equal with God, and for this they would've stoned him (John 5:18).

So is Jesus who he claimed to be? Notice Jesus really did make those claims personally. I'm emphasizing that because some have taken the view that the Jesus of history and the Jesus of faith are two different things. As if Jesus' followers exaggerated matters out of all proportion to reality. A more common opinion is that Jesus did exist, and was a good man, a good moral teacher, one whose views are to be respected. But is that position credible? Remember Jesus himself claimed to be the Son of God. Good men don't tell lies. Jesus claimed to be the Son of God. Either that claim is true or it's false. If it's true, then he is who he claimed to be – he's Lord. But if his claim to be the Son of God was false, then, it is worth reiterating once again that there are only two possibilities.

Either he knew he was making a false claim – and so he's a liar or else he made a false claim without realizing it was false – now, if you think you're the Son of God when you're not, you must be a lunatic. So these are the only possibilities: Lord, liar or lunatic. Jesus could not have been only a good man. The historical record of Jesus' life – and the profound and lasting impact it's had around the world ever since - is one of the strongest, if not the strongest, evidence for the existence of God. His was a life so powerful it reset the clocks 2,000 years ago, meaning that we date our calendar from his birth.

Across the centuries and cultures, the life of Christ stands supreme and impeccable. Atheist Bertrand Russell admitted that it was debatable wh ether the method adopted by Mahatma Gandhi when calling for Indian independence from British rule would have succeeded, except for the fact that it appealed to the conscience of a nation that had been influenced by the gospel. Today, in the city of Ahmedabad in central India, Russell's quotation greets each visitor. How remarkable is that! In a predominantly Hindu nation, a quote by an atheist testifies to the impact of Christ upon both East and West in the world today! Such has been the impact of 'a life so well lived' that it's felt around the world, in all its cultures. That unique testimony to the lasting impact through history of one short life brings us back to Jesus' claim to be God's Son. We've argued that the question of his identity is bound up together with the understanding that Jesus' miracles were totally authentic supernatural events. Taken at face-value, the miracles themselves were the credentials he presented in support of his claim to be the Jewish Messiah, the Son of God.

We see this is the case when to the Jews, Jesus proclaimed, "The very works [meaning miracles] that I do bear witness of Me, that the Father has sent Me." These works he described as being those that his Father had given him to accomplish. It is clear then that he viewed them as his credentials to a disbelieving nation.

The supreme credentials, of course, were the greatest miracles of all – his miraculous virgin birth and his resurrection. They're at once reasonable if we accept that God exists – the God who has created all things. US chat show host, Larry King, was once asked whom he would most like to interview from across all the centuries. Among the names he put forward was that of Jesus Christ. The interviewer couldn't resist: "Mr. King, what question would you want to put to Jesus Christ?" Larry King replied, "I would ask him if he really was virgin-born -because the answer to that question defines history." He was absolutely right. For we're dealing here with an event that defines reality – that defines truth. The person of Jesus Christ is the last of four evidences for the existence of God which the Apostle Paul mentions at the beginning of his Bible letter to the Romans (Creation (1:20); Conscience (2:15); Communication (3:2); Christ (3:24).

All that we've said stands or falls together. The case for God's existence is entirely reasonable. And from that starting point we can go on to accept that he's come down into human history in the person of Jesus Christ; coming for the very purpose of dying on that Roman cross just outside Jerusalem as a sacrifice for our sins. Suffering, dying, and rising again victorious from the dead in the power of God on the third day – perhaps the greatest miracle of all. The existence of God, the identity of Jesus Christ, the status of his miracles: all three of these belong together – each reasonable because it draws support from the others.

Remember the thief in our opening illustration – he wasn't a prisoner to the laws of arithmetic when he stole the money. And neither was God a prisoner to the laws of nature when he became a glorious intruder into our history through the miracle-working Jesus Christ. God in Christ has visited us to provide a way back to himself for us. A way made necessary, because the Bible teaches that humanity, made in the image of God, fell morally and spiritually through original disobedience from perfection. This is the miracle of divine love: that God's Son came to die that we might have eternal life in him. This is the only way of salvation: simply by trusting in his shed blood. By His sacrificial death, accepted personally in faith, we are delivered from God's wrath which our sins deserve.

This Jesus who died, God has made both Lord and Christ. He is above all authority and there is a time coming when all in the tombs shall hear his voice, for he is the Resurrection and the Life. His resurrection is the assurance of future judgement, as he will sit as the Judge. How will you face him in that day? If you have not done so already, admit you are a sinner, turn from your sin, believe on the Lord Jesus, who came to save you through his death, and receive him as your personal Saviour.

CHAPTER FOURTEEN: "THE BIBLE IS FULL OF ERRORS AND CONTRADICTIONS"

Christians believe the Bible is ultimate truth; that it's God's Word for the human race; that in it the Creator has communicated with his creatures. There are people whose hearts are set against believing that. This chapter is not aimed at them, for they've no wish to be persuaded. But I've met many people – and I'm sure you have too – who quite casually say, "You can't trust the Bible. It's full of errors and contradictions." In my experience, when I try to engage them in conversation, I find that they are simply repeating something they've heard someone else say. I honestly don't think some who say this have actually ever sat down and read the Bible. So why do they say it? Often, I suspect, they use it as a way to avoid having to think about what are, for them, uncomfortable issues, such as their accountability to God.

Perhaps someone has voiced the objection to you, "But isn't the Bible full of errors?" How did you respond? Or it could be that you have doubts of your own. Either way, I hope this chapter will be of some help. Sometimes the sincerity of those who make this criticism is immediately suspect, for when asked for an example, they can't furnish a single one. Some may claim some alleged evidence. However, apparent contradictions there may be, but when we rightly understand the historical and scientific facts presented in the Bible (and for this we need the help of the Spirit of God), and when we also rightly interpret the historical and scientific facts from the world around us, we see there's no contradiction after all. Sir William Ramsay, who devoted many years to the archaeology of Asia Minor, has testified to Luke's intimate and accurate acquaintance with Asia Minor and the Greek East at that time. Although in his later years Ramsay came to be a champion for the trustworthiness of the New Testament records, his were judgments which he had previously formed as a scientific archaeologist and student of ancient classical history and literature.

When he said, "Luke's history is unsurpassed in respect of its trustworthiness," it was the conclusion his researches had led him to, in spite of the fact that he started with a very different opinion. He put it: 'Luke is a historian of the first rank ... this author should be placed along with the very greatest of historians." Ramsay overcame his prejudice. For whatever reason, he had at first been disinclined to accept the reliability of the Bible as history – until he brought his relevant expertise to bear on the actual evidence. In fact, an outstanding Jewish archaeologist has stated that 'no archaeological discovery has ever controverted a biblical reference.' On the contrary, there have been discoveries that have completely vindicated the Bible. Characters, stories and books of the Bible which were once dismissed by critics, must now be taken more seriously by them as a result of evidence from outside the Bible which is consistent with the siege of Jericho, the walled-city, with David the great king of Israel, and with the historical setting of the Book of Daniel – to name a few.

Careful historical and archeological and scientific research time after time ends up vindicating the Bible. An article by Dr. Alan R. Millard appeared in *Biblical Archaeology Review* (May/June, 1985). At the time, Millard was a Senior Lecturer in Hebrew and Ancient Semitic Languages at the University of Liverpool, England. He explains there about the discovery of clay cylinders in southern Iraq by J.G. Taylor. A man called Sir Henry

Rawlinson was able to read the Babylonian inscriptions on them which had been written at the command of Nabonidus, king of Babylon from 555 to 539BC. The words were a prayer for the long life and good health of Nabonidus - and for his eldest son. And the name of that son, clearly written, was Belshazzar! What's the significance of that, you might ask?

The Bible book of Daniel has been one of the books unbelievers and critics have targetted most. One of their strongest arguments against it being genuine was in claiming that such a character as Belshazzar never existed – since, they thought, he was unknown to history. Historians were sure Nabonidus was the last Babylonian king, and that he was absent from the city when it was captured. The conclusion was the Belshazzar was mythical and the whole story of Daniel could be dismissed as legendary. However, that was before those clay cylinders were found at Chaldean sites which mentioned Belshazzar as being the eldest son of Nabonidus. Doubtless then, he reigned as regent in the city during his father's absences. This would have made him the second ruler (co-regent) in the kingdom and explains the seemingly strange piece of information given that he appointed Daniel as the third ruler in the kingdom (Daniel 5:16).

Here is clear proof that an important person named Belshazzar lived in Babylon during the last years of the city's independence. So Belshazzar was not an imaginary figure after all. In some of the inscriptions discovered from the reign of Nabonidus, we find that the parties swear by Nabonidus and by Belshazzar, the king's son. This suggests that Belshazzar may well have had a special status. We know that during part of his father's reign, Belshazzar was the effective authority in Babylon. According to one account, Nabonidus 'entrusted the kingship' to Belshazzar (*BAR* 11:03, May/June 1985). As Belshazzar was already second in the kingdom, serving as a co-regent with his absent father, he could offer Daniel nothing greater than to become 'third ruler in the kingdom.'

It's easy to dismiss something if we refuse to even consider taking its claims seriously. But if we're sincere, and take the challenge to investigate properly then we, too, may be surprised. But external evidence is not the only test which the Bible passes. Another test of any piece of ancient literature is what might be called the 'internal test'. Basically, this test asks the question: 'Does it ring true?' Take, for example, the fact that the writers of the four Gospels write about themselves and their companions in ways that are far from flattering. Their failures are highlighted. Like Peter's shameful denial of Jesus, and the doubts Thomas had. We get to see them 'warts and all,' as it were. As when they're cowering for fear in that upper room in Jerusalem and describe their own total shock when Jesus appeared to them in resurrection. There's a very real sense we're seeing the story as it truly happened. They write of an event they were unprepared for. Of course someone might say 'but this is just creative writing'. Think it through the whole way. We do know that not a few of these early writers - and other Christians - died a martyr's death. It's one thing to willingly accept death for something you passionately and sincerely believe in – but who would die for a lie? Who would die for a creative fabrication of their own making?

But just suppose, for the sake of argument, that you want to persist in believing that these men were living a lie and making the whole thing up. If that was their motive, and they were being as careful as you give them credit for being, then surely they wouldn't have introduced elements into the story which defied the conventions and customs of the society in which they lived. They would never have done that if they were desperately trying to be convincing. But in the unfolding drama, as recorded, of the resurrection, it's women who play a leading role as the first witnesses. They're prominent in the early record. Now bear in mind that, at this point in history and in that culture especially, the testimony of women was not considered valid in a court of law. The Jewish religious leaders didn't talk with women – apart from their own wives presumably. So why weaken your own case? Why did they say women were the earliest witnesses – unless that's exactly how it was.

But those who at least have a superficial acquaintance with the Bible may point to two Bible references to the same incident which appear to give different information, for example one account saying two blind beggars were healed by Jesus; while the other record mentions only one. Fair enough, but there's no impossible contradiction is there? If there were two, then there most certainly was one. It's natural for eyewitnesses to focus down on different things. That's common in any court of law. It's even more common when you have spectators comparing views on a football match they've both watched together. You sometimes wonder if they really did see the same match, but of course you know they did. Now, there's one third and final test, alongside the external and internal tests we've thought about already. In the case of all ancient documents, we no longer have the originals. The materials they were written down on wore out long ago. But copies were made, and then these also were copied, and so the record of ancient events was passed down to us. This is true not only of the Bible, but also of, the record of Caesar's Gallic Wars, for example. So we only have copies of copies of copies. How, then, do the experts have confidence in what is reliable and what is not?

They gather up all the copies in existence and find out the date of the oldest copy. They then compare that date with the date of the original writing. If there are lots of copies and if the time gap between the original and the oldest existing copy is small, then that gives a high degree of confidence that the copies we have are reliable. For example, in the case of the record of his Gallic Wars by Julius Caesar we have 10 copies known to us today, and they date back to 1,000 years after Caesar's death. On the strength of that, these documentary writings are believed to be trustworthy by historians. So that gives us a feel for the standard that's acceptable to those who routinely deal with these things. So now let's turn to the New Testament of the Bible. We find that lots of really old copies of what was written still survive – there are literally thousands of manuscripts in differing degrees of completeness – and dating back to only a hundred years or so since the time of the cross of Christ. So by the same standards, to a fair-minded person, who's really looking into the evidence, the Bible has to be accepted as an accurate record of events – at least if we accept any other piece of ancient literature, then we must accept the Bible.

I know it may seem confusing that there are so many differences in translated versions of the Bible today, but these differences are really not down to disagreement between the existing copies made from the original, but they reflect different styles of translation. While some variations exist, there's an 'overwhelming degree of agreement which exists among the ancient records'. The bottom line is we can have confidence in the Bible we hold in our hands today. This fact was reinforced in 1947 with the discovery of the Dead Sea scrolls. These scrolls found well-preserved in a cave were found to contain copies of Bible books like that of the prophet Isaiah which were a thousand years older than any other copy previously known to exist. And when they made the comparisons, they confirmed that there had been accurate copying. In fact, we know that the care taken in copying by hand was almost unbelievable with very many detailed cross-checks being made. And what the Dead Sea scrolls prove is that the system worked amazingly well! For the Jews involved of course believed they were handling a sacred text.

But the Bible makes claims that the original writings were 'God-breathed' or inspired by God, a supernatural process which guided the 40 or so human authors over some one-and-a-half-thousand years. Is there anything testable which backs up that claim? The fulfilled prophecies found in the Bible are the proof that it's the inspired Word of God. For example, over 300 prophecies about the Messiah were exactly fulfilled in Jesus Christ. Some predictions were so improbable of fulfilment that no human insight could ever have foreseen them. If you read Matthew's Gospel, you'll discover a dozen specific ways the life of Jesus satisfied the Old Testament predictions for the one who had come as the Jewish Messiah. Isaiah, writing around 700 years before Christ's birth, foretold of Jesus that as the Messiah he'd be despised and rejected and suffer terribly (Isaiah 53). It was an incredible portrait he painted of his own nation not recognizing, but rejecting their own Messiah for whom they were longingly waiting. But, amazing as it was, we know it came true in Jesus' life and death. The evidence for the Bible being the Word of God, and Jesus being the Son of God, is overwhelming. The purpose of this divinely inspired book is that you may believe Jesus is God's Son, and, by believing, have life in his Name.

CHAPTER FIFTEEN: "IT'S NONSENSE TO BELIEVE IN HELL AND A GOD OF LOVE!"

I'm sure you've heard this objection, usually when Christians preach the love God commended towards us in that Jesus died for us to save us from the just penalty which our sins deserve, namely the lake of fire. Ah, the lake of fire: that's the cue for this objection: "You've just claimed that God's a God of love," they say, "but now you talk of hell-fire. How is it possible to believe in hell and a God of love? Surely," they continue, "if God really was a loving God he wouldn't send anyone to the lake of fire forever." There seems to be some force to it at first hearing, doesn't there?

But I doubt if those who raise this objection have ever stopped to analyse their own assumptions – the assumptions which are hidden within this objection they're making? Can you see what the questioner is assuming? They are assuming that there's something obviously wrong with the idea of God, especially a so-called loving God, sending anyone to the lake of fire. The hidden assumption is that this is somehow immoral. No loving being would ever do such a thing! Now, it could be worth asking the questioner where this sense of morality, this gut feeling about the rights and wrongs of the situation, comes from. Jesus himself used the technique of questioning his questioners. It's not a game, but it can show the questioner the deeper issues that lie behind his own question – and so perhaps test his or her sincerity. Have they thought this through, or is it a second-hand objection, conveniently wheeled out to avoid talk of God and of our accountability to him? It's especially relevant to do this if we suspect this objection is not the result of someone struggling with weak faith, but if we think the questioner really is implying that they have found in this objection a satisfying reason for not believing in God at all.

A totally consistent atheist does not acknowledge the existence of evil, and claims not to recognize the difference between right and wrong. I've heard of this being taken to extremes in a debate between a philosopher who was an atheist and another philosopher who was a Christian. The atheist objected to the Christian's use of the term evil. Why? Well, if he were to accept such a thing as evil existed, then good must also exist, for there's got to be a contrast whereby the one helps define the other, as being its opposite. But then if both evil and good exist, then it stands to reason that there are a whole lot of in-between values – some things not as good as other things – degrees of evil, if you like. In other words we end up with a whole spectrum arranged according to some sort of scale of values. That means we must have a moral scale, a kind of yardstick with which we intuitively measure morality or how good or evil some event is. But to have such a moral law also presumes there's a Giver of that moral law – which is, of course, what the Bible claims is indeed the case.

Back to our atheist philosopher who, naturally enough, wanted to side-step that logic by denying the existence of evil. He said 'evil' was a meaningless term for him. It's just a label that gets used by society for things which we don't like. The Christian philosopher decided to put the atheist's view to the test. 'Imagine there's a young child, a baby, lying here in front of us,' he said. 'If I, or someone else, were to take a huge kitchen knife, and cut that innocent baby in pieces, would you not admit that would be an evil thing to do?' All eyes in the audience were now fixed on the atheist. 'I would not like that to happen,' he said, 'but I could not describe it as being an evil act.' There was a gasp from the audience. There were probably many who, before then, had not seen the existence of evil as actually presenting evidence for the existence of God. There was no question about who'd won the debate.

You remember we were talking about the objection to the Christian message which goes like this: 'How can you believe in hell and also in a God of love?' We were saying it's worth exposing the hidden assumption in the question which somehow implies it's immoral for a loving God to punish persons in the lake of fire. The point is by assuming some basis for morality (and so 'evil') – however imperfect in their understanding – they've actually fatally weakened any case against God's existence they may have thought they had. But some objectors may accept that there is a God, while refusing to consider it a reasonable thing for such a God to send anyone to eternal punishment. If they believe in God, they very likely will also accept that Jesus Christ was at least a good man, a great moral teacher. We should then focus on the person of Jesus Christ. He's presented in the New Testament of the Bible as someone who went about doing good; always helping people in difficulty, demonstrating more than anyone else the love of his Father, God ... but he – more than anyone else in the Bible – was a hell-fire preacher!

The Bible's account of his life – which is consistent with sources outside the Bible, and indeed with the impact of his life around the world ever since – the Bible account of his life shows him to have been the kindest and truest of men. The issue of hell and a God of love comes into sharp focus in the person of Jesus Christ himself. He, the kindest and truest of men, taught repeatedly about the reality of hell; of the judgement to come. Jesus spoke of hell some twelve times as recorded in the four Gospels. Was he being untrue or unkind on those occasions? That doesn't fit at all. Much rather, because of who he is, and because of what he's like, he was giving fair warning to all so that we might by God's grace escape such a fearful reality as eternal punishment in the lake of fire.

It was because of his perfect knowledge of the reality of hell that Jesus came down in love to earth, to make possible, through his death for our sins, a way of escape for all who believe on him. The Bible says that 'all have sinned', and that this inevitably leads to 'death', for God must punish sin. Death, as we understand it in a physical sense here on earth, brings separation and feelings of remoteness and alienation. This is the essence of eternal death in the lake of fire: total separation and alienation from God. Jesus spoke of this final state - using such descriptions as 'eternal fire', 'outer darkness' and 'place of weeping'. These portray to us at least an agonising awareness of God's wrath, together with a total sense of loss and separation and self-loathing.

Thank God that all who accept Jesus as Saviour will never suffer this fate. But those who refuse to believe on Christ will die in their sins and where he is they cannot go. It couldn't be fairer — God will honour for eternity what we choose now. In the light of this, if you haven't before, please take this opportunity of accepting Jesus now as your personal Saviour. He died on the cross to take your punishment instead of you, if you'll only repent and believe.

I know it's not popular to speak of punishment today, whether it's God's eternal punishment of sinners who refuse to believe in Christ's sacrifice for them, or just plain ordinary punishment within society. We much prefer to treat people instead of punish people nowadays. However, the reality is actually the very opposite of what our questioner thinks is fair. In real terms, there can be no loving justice for all unless there is punishment.

I was reminded of this when on the 26th of April, 2007, the verdict was announced in the Lucie Blackman murder trial in Japan. On that same morning, in the BBC radio's Today programme, on 'Thought for the Day', Anne Atkins spoke about a paradox. On the one hand, the accused had been found guilty and given a life sentence: on the other hand, the victim's family was still devastated at the verdict. Why? Because at that time he had not been found guilty of crimes specifically committed against her. But what's the point of them demanding more? Joji Obara already had a life sentence. The point, we were reminded, was Lucie. She was beautiful, she was young, she was loved. A dreadful sin was committed against her. If that isn't addressed, there's a slur on her worth.

I mention this because some say, "Why shouldn't God simply forgive every one of us – of all our wrongs against each other?' Well, if God simply forgave everyone without demonstrating justice, he would be suggesting that all the Lucies who have ever suffered injustice in the world don't matter. But they do matter. We all matter to God, and the point is our sins – meaning all our wrongs, not just crimes – devalue others, as well as offending God. So many times our thoughts demean, our words belittle. That's why on the appointed day to come, God will address with total justice the wrongs which have been done. But there's good news: Jesus Christ, whose life as a man showed him to be actually more than a man, paid for human sin on the cross where he died. His words and the Bible's claims clearly declare him to be God's son, sharing our humanity for the deliberate purpose of dying sacrificially in order to satisfy God's justice on account of our sins. For us to receive forgiveness on this basis – which is both loving and just – all God asks us to do is to turn from our self-centred, self-choosing, self-serving ways and trust fully in his son, Jesus Christ, who served our sentence in his death on the cross for our sins.

CHAPTER SIXTEEN: "SCIENCE HAS ELIMINATED THE NEED FOR FAITH"

I have had the experience of being met with a patronizing smile after raising 'the God issue' in a conversation. Many of those we talk to seem to make the assumption that science has done away with the need for faith. It's an understandable reaction. Scientific figures in the media spotlight have popularized certain scientific ideas in a way that makes them appear hostile to any faith in God. Take, for example, what we noted earlier that Stephen Jay Gould, lately of Harvard had to say about human origins:

'We are here because one odd group of fishes had a peculiar fin anatomy that could transform into legs for terrestrial creatures; because comets struck the earth and wiped out dinosaurs, thereby giving mammals a chance not otherwise available (so thank your lucky stars in a literal sense); because the earth never froze entirely during an ice age; because a small and tenuous species, arising in Africa a quarter of a million years ago, has managed, so far, to survive by hook and by crook. We may yearn for a "higher" answer - but none exists. This explanation, though superficially troubling ... is ultimately ... exhilarating.'

Most people hearing that would tend to think 'that man is a scientific expert; he really knows what he's talking about. So as weird as it may sound, it must be true.' Tragically, they may conclude that modern scientific understanding of how things really are, has done away with any need to believe in a Creator God - God has been replaced by 'time and chance', and no 'higher' answer exists. This conclusion is what Stephen Jay Gould finds exhilarating, although I confess I'm at a loss to understand why. Why should the idea that we're simply the random products of mere chance in a purposeless existence be in any way, shape or form, exhilarating? But there again, an eminent professor has said it and so many people, hearing it spoken with such conviction, will take it on trust that all he says has been established by science. But has it? Is this fact or mere speculation?

Perhaps the most convincing way to demonstrate that it's speculation – and not fact - is to use the words of one of the world's most outspoken atheists today – someone who would, of course, totally agree with Stephen Jay Gould's sentiment. I'm talking about Richard Dawkins, of course. He's always trumpeting the need to take an evidence-based approach to everything, to such an extent, that someone was once moved to ask him if there was anything he believed in without being able to prove it. His answer was both candid and illuminating. He said, "I believe, but I cannot prove, that all life, all intelligence, all creativity and all 'design' anywhere in the universe, is the direct or indirect product of Darwinian natural selection" (Dawkins quoted in the book *Letter from a Christian Citizen* by Douglas Wilson, AV Press, 2007, in the foreward, p.xviii).

That, surprisingly enough, is a very fair statement. Dawkins is well known in the western world for his anti-God rhetoric. He's the kind of person the media would tend to turn to, to ask for a scientific perspective. But here, in his own words, he's candid enough to say that what he holds is, in fact, a faith position. Of course, this must be so, if you think about it, as no theory of origins can be scientifically proved, for we weren't around back then. All the evidence available to us to observe and test exists, of course, in the present. It's only by one indirect means or another that we can infer from it something about the past. It's not something that can be done directly, so theories about the past must always be based on assumptions – and that's really another way of talking about beliefs. Michael Polanyi has gone so far as to state that human reason never operates in a vacuum – it never operates outside of a framework of basic beliefs. This means that to admit faith as being necessary to understanding something of creation is not different in principle from the usual way science operates. And indeed many famous scientists found a place for God in the framework of basic beliefs which supported their scientific research. This shows there's no conflict between science and religion; but only between the two opposed worldviews of naturalism and theism.

For example, Johannes Kepler who discovered the three laws of planetary motion said that to him the universe was a 'sacred sermon, a veritable hymn to God the Creator'. He added: 'O God, I am thinking Thy thoughts after Thee'. These men were the giants of the world of science. We only see further today than they saw, because we stand on their shoulders. Today, Stephen Hawking, who sits in Sir Isaac Newton's chair at Cambridge University in the UK, is one of the best-known theoretical physicists of his generation. He has done ground-breaking research on 'black holes' (volumes of space from which no light can escape – having been trapped by a very massive object). But he poses a vital question when he asks: 'What is it that breathes fire into the equations and makes a universe for them to describe?' The fact that one of the brightest minds in science is asking the question, shows us that this is a type of question which science itself isn't able to answer. Science is basically all about asking, "How?" How the heavenly bodies move as they do. How various substances will react with one another. But science can't begin to answer the 'why' question: the fundamental question of why things are as they are. Science at best attempts a description of reality, but why reality should be as it is, is a different kind of question – a deeper, philosophical question.

And so we get into philosophical arguments based on the fact that every event has a cause, or – more carefully – that every thing that has a beginning must have a cause.

The argument goes like this:

1. Whatever begins to exist has a cause.

2. The universe began to exist.

3. Therefore, the universe must have a cause.

Probably, most reasonable people would refuse to accept that the universe sprang into existence 'uncaused' out of nothing. Following the so-called 'Big Bang' theory, as we run the clocks backward in time we arrive at a point where the laws of science, as we know them today, break down. Put another way, what that means is not even scientists have a scientific explanation for what happened right at the beginning of time! So there's no need to be in any way embarrassed by the majestic statement with which the Bible opens: 'In the beginning God ...'

As the world-class philosopher Alvin Plantinga has said: all explanations have to end somewhere. Materialists equally have no explanation for the existence of elementary particles: in their view they simply are. Scientific evidence which is consistent with there having been an actual beginning comes from a very basic and general law of science (known as the Second Law of Thermodynamics) which lies behind the fact that everything we see around us is gradually wearing out, implying there was a time when it was once 'brand new'. And so it's at least reasonable to argue, although perhaps not to everyone's satisfaction, that the universe, since it once began to exist, must also have a cause for its existence at the time it began. Christianity then asserts that the great uncaused First Cause of all things is the God of the Bible –

which begins by answering the 'why' question which science can't answer. 'In the beginning God created the heavens and the earth'.

We choose to believe that (accepting it, on God's own authority, from his Word, the Bible) – in a way that's really no different from the scientist who chooses to believe in chance. Faith is the only way we can prove God, faith is the proving of things not seen (see Hebrews 11:1,2). But this is not blind faith. There's evidence to support this faith. The things that are seen, give reasonable evidence for that starting point of faith (see Romans 1:20). In fact, the ultimate reality is that we are without excuse if we wilfully refuse to have God in our knowledge. Maybe the point can be brought home if we return the challenge – by asking our challenger if he or she can disprove God's existence. If they dared to claim they could, then what they're in effect claiming is that they've got infinite knowledge – for before I could even claim that no such thing as say, a rainbow-coloured stone exists anywhere in the universe, technically I'd need to know – ultimately by visiting – that in every possible location in the universe no such stone is to be found. Far less can anyone hope to prove that God does not exist. "And without faith it is impossible to please Him, for he who comes to God must believe that He is and that He is a rewarder of those who seek Him" (Hebrews 11:6).

CHAPTER SEVENTEEN: "ALL THE BLOODSHED IN THE NAME OF RELIGION IS JUST HYPOCRISY"

One of the popular comebacks when talking to people about the Christian faith is to hear people respond and say 'Oh, don't talk to me about religion! What about all the blood that's been shed in the name of religion?' Often they'll add: 'There's been more blood shed in the name of religion than for any other reason.' Often it's a tactic to close down the conversation, but let's at least take the challenge seriously. I wonder if the person who raises this objection has ever sat down and really tried to estimate the number of people who have been killed by irreligion?

I know how people in the west tend to throw up the example of the Spanish Inquisition as an example of religious horror – and that's perfectly understandable. We should first point out that we are not in the business of defending it. But to put even that horror into perspective, what about comparing it with the scientific socialism of Communist countries which have killed 100 million (and still counting) around the globe? It's reckoned that Stalin alone may have been responsible for an estimated 30 million of those deaths. This is the Stalin who abandoned his seminary training and began to dogmatically deny the existence of God. But his daughter Svetlana said that her father when he was dying, sat up one final time from his death-bed and shook his fist at the ceiling. One has to wonder who he was shaking his fist at. But if we go back for a moment to the Inquisition which in the course of three centuries, killed perhaps 3,000 people, what we find – as we put even that horror into perspective – is that this was fewer people than the Soviet Union killed on an average day.

There again, the scientific racism of Nazi Germany killed 40 million – and attempted genocide against Europe's Jews. It's well enough documented that this was the out-working of anti-God ideas – the result of irreligious philosophies. The nineteenth century German philosopher, Frederick Nietsche (d.1900), had wanted to dismantle what he saw as the scaffolding effect of Christianity upon society. He felt that Christian morality stood in the way of progress. What Nietsche wanted to do was to try an alternative foundation, a foundation without God. It was Nietsche who made popular the statement 'God is dead' – and dramatically portrayed it in his parable called The Madman, which goes like this:

'Have you not heard of that madman who lit a lantern in the bright morning hours, ran to the marketplace and cried incessantly, "I'm looking for God, I'm looking for God!" As many of those who did not believe in God were standing there, he excited considerable laughter. "Why, did he get lost?" said one. "Did he lose his way like a child?" said another. "Or is he hiding? Is he afraid of us? Has he gone on a voyage? Or emigrated?" Thus they yelled and laughed. The madman sprang into their midst and pierced them with his glances. "Whither is God?" he cried. "I shall tell you. We have killed him – you and I. All of us are his murderers ... God is dead, and we have killed him."

When Nietsche was talking about killing God, he meant killing God philosophically, of course. He had little idea how costly this attempt would be in terms of human deaths. First of all, in his own life and health. Because, for the last dozen or so years of his life he himself became the madman. Then along came his fellow-countryman, Hitler, to put Nietsche's ideas into practice and to build on them. The world soon learnt of the horrors that follow when we de-construct the foundations of good thinking, and begin to build instead on the basic idea that God is dead, and life is senseless. Nietsche in the 19th century actually forecast madness and violence in the 20th century based on the acceptance of his philosophy. This was fulfilled when Hitler gave copies of Nietsche's work to Stalin and Mussolini. And when Hitler and Stalin built on these ideas, applying them to the fundamental values of society, disaster unfolded. As we say, Nazi Germany killed 40 million and Communist countries killed 100 million – all in the name of irreligion. Those who claim more bloodshed has taken place in the name of religion than anything else seem to have forgotten the terrible lesson from these fearful social experiments of the twentieth century.

And it's precisely these social experiments that support the Christian claim that the moral absolutes of the Bible are the best foundation for life! As Jesus said: "Therefore everyone who hears these words of Mine and acts on them, may be compared to a wise man who built his house on the rock. And the rain fell, and the floods came, and the winds blew and slammed against that house; and yet it did not fall, for it had been founded on the rock. Everyone who hears these words of Mine and does not act on them, will be like a foolish man who built his house on the sand. The rain fell, and the floods came, and the winds blew and slammed against that house; and it fell - and great was its fall" (Matthew 7:24-27).

By the way, we fully accept that religious bigotry is a horrible and cruel thing. There's no way we would wish to be thought of as defending it. After all, it was religious bigotry that put Christ on the cross. That now brings us to emphasize the difference between religion and faith. Religion is all about trying to do what we think we can do for God; whereas the essence of the Christian faith is all about what God has done for us – in giving his own Son to die for our sins at the cross. Christianity is a living faith in a personal relationship with God through Jesus Christ. So we are not really in the business of defending what's been done in the name of religion in any case.

On the contrary, we would make the case that a genuine experience of Christianity that's truly Bible-based, is perceived today as not carrying the threat of violence, but rather being a force for peace in an increasingly violent world. In a public debate, the Oxford atheistic philosopher Jonathan Glover was asked: 'If you, Professor Glover, were stranded at the midnight hour in a desolate Los Angeles street and if, as you stepped out of your car with fear and trembling, you were suddenly to hear the weight of pounding footsteps behind you, and you saw ten burly young men who had just stepped out of a dwelling coming towards you, would it or would it not make a difference to you to know that they were coming from a Bible study?' While the audience laughed, the professor admitted it would make a difference.

Of course, the same could not be said of all world religions today, but that's to come back to the clear distinction we're making between what's done in the name of some religion and what's consistent with the true expression of biblical Christian faith. Christianity has a proven track record of changing violent, blood-thirsty people into peace-loving citizens. One of the most gripping examples of a changed life which I've come across recently is the story of Stephen Lungu. He tells it in his book 'Out of the Black Shadows'. The Black Shadows being the gang he ran with in Zimbabwe, back in the days in which it was called Rhodesia. Rejected by his father, and abandoned by his mother when they split up, Stephen grew up with an angry and bitter heart. One night he and his gang-members decided to petrol bomb a mission tent where a preacher was addressing hundreds of people. He made the mistake of first stopping to listen for a few minutes. He describes in his book how the preacher jabbed with his pointed finger: 'all have sinned'; 'the wages of sin is death', adding 'some here are not ready to die tonight'.

Misunderstanding that, Stephen couldn't work out how this preacher already seemed to know about their plans to kill as many people as possible in the tent that night. Well, the preacher that night went on to speak about how Jesus became poor that we might become rich. Stephen could relate to poverty all right, and quite fancied exchanging it for riches, so clutching his bag of petrol bombs, he was soon moving, almost involuntarily, to the front in a state of emotional and spiritual turmoil. The meeting was then interrupted when others started the petrol bomb attack which Stephen had meant to lead. At that point the preacher acknowledged Stephen's presence before him. "Can your Jesus save someone like me?" Stephen asked. "Yes," came the reply along with a request to share a bit of Stephen's background information.

As Stephen told of his early rejection, the preacher himself began to cry. "Young man," he said, "I shall now tell you a story. Many years ago there was a 14-year-old girl who became pregnant." He went on to tell of how the father refused to take responsibility, so the girl dumped the baby in a toilet, but someone heard it drowning and rescued it, taking it to hospital. "I was that child," the preacher said. Stephen stared at him in astonishment. The preacher then read to him Psalm 27:10: 'Though my father and my mother forsake me, the Lord will take me up.' Hearing that verse became the changing point in Stephen's life. "God," he cried, "I have nothing. I am nothing. I can't read. I can't write. My parents don't want me. Take me up,

God, take me up. I'm sorry for the bad things I've done. Jesus, forgive me, and take me now'.

A throw-away child among the millions of Africa, but Jesus had found him – and turned his life round. To this day he tells others, all across Africa and beyond, of how God took him up. I pray this little book may be of some little help under God in equipping us to answer the critics, so that in the power of God they might be turned from their cynicism to a vibrant faith in Jesus Christ.

CHAPTER EIGHTEEN: "THERE'S NO SUCH THING AS OBJECTIVE TRUTH"

Sometimes an unscheduled conversation with a stranger can surface life's big questions. Let's revisit one we've recounted earlier. An Oxford professor who was a mathematician, boarded a train and sat down next to a fellow-passenger. Glancing up, the newcomer saw that the papers the man was reading were of a scientific nature. "I see you're a scientist," he said by way of opening a conversation. "Yes, I'm a metallurgist ... and yourself?" "I'm a mathematician." Then silence descended upon the travellers until the mathematician pulled out a copy of the New Testament and began to read. The metallurgist strained his neck to see the book the mathematician was reading. The latter obliged by making it easier to see. "Excuse me, the scientist said when he could contain his curiosity no longer, but you did say you were a mathematician, didn't you?" "Yes, that's right." "But you're reading the New Testament!" "I am," and sensing his companion was struggling somehow to reconcile the two facts, the mathematician added, "May I ask you something?" Permission was granted, so he asked: "Tell me, do you have any hope?" "I guess we'll all muddle through." The mathematician put down his New Testament, "but that's not what I really asked," he said. "Do you have any personal hope?" "None whatsoever," was the follow-up reply. "Would you like a copy of the New Testament?" "Yes, maybe I will, thanks."

The New Testament of the Bible, a copy of which was handed over that day, points to a personal hope that extends beyond the grave for those who receive its message. We're told: "... whatever was written in earlier times was written for our instruction, so that through perseverance and the encouragement of the Scriptures we might have hope" (Romans 15:4).

And at a time when the apostle Paul was defending his Christianity, he said: "... I am on trial for the hope and resurrection of the dead!" (Acts 23:6). So such a personal hope that stretches beyond the grave is a major, defining feature of Biblical Christianity. Again, Paul shows this by talking about "having a hope in God ... that there will be a resurrection of both the just and the unjust" (Acts 24:15)

Christianity gives hope. To believe in God is to believe in immortality: to believe in a resurrection where we'll face an assessment of our life. It's this broader framework that does more than lift life beyond the level of a farce – which was the best one notable scientist said he could hope for through devoting himself to scientific endeavours. The eternal perspective which belief in God and immortality gives us, not only brings with it a sense of absolute values, but also brings moral accountability. It fills our life with meaning so that we can live for more than ourselves – and all this without having to pretend to invent a Noble Lie to give us something beyond ourselves to live for.

I'm reminded of another train journey – this time one by Albert Einstein, the great scientist, honoured by Time magazine as the Man of the last Century. Einstein was once travelling from Princeton on a train, when the ticket inspector came down the aisle, checking the tickets of each passenger. When he came to the row of seats where Einstein was sitting, the absent-minded professor reached into his jacket pocket. He couldn't find his ticket there, so he tried his other pockets. It wasn't in any of them, so he searched for it in his briefcase, but still couldn't find it. He even searched the empty seat next to him. No good, still no ticket.

The ticket inspector said, "Dr. Einstein, I know who you are. We all know who you are. I'm sure you bought a ticket. Don't worry about it." Einstein nodded appreciatively. The ticket inspector continued on his way down the aisle, checking tickets. As he was ready to move to the next compartment of the train, he turned around and saw that the great scientist down on his hands and knees, looking under his seat for the ticket.

The inspector rushed back and said, "Dr. Einstein, Dr. Einstein, don't worry, I know who you are. No problem. You don't need a ticket. I'm sure you bought one." Einstein looked at him and said, "Young man, I too, know who I am. What I don't know is where I'm going." The absent-minded professor needed to re-read the destination printed on his ticket in order to remember where he was going and the purpose of the journey he was on! Not knowing where they were going was also the issue for Jesus' first disciples to whom Jesus said:

"In My Father's house are many dwelling places; if it were not so, I would have told you; for I go to prepare a place for you. If I go and prepare a place for you, I will come again and receive you to Myself, that where I am, there you may be also. And you know the way where I am going." Thomas said to Him, "Lord, we do not know where You are going, how do we know the way?" Jesus said to him, "I am the way, and the truth, and the life; no one comes to the Father but through Me" (John 14:2-6).

Very often today you find a reaction against exclusive claims like that. In the mood of much of the modern world such exclusive claims are regarded as unacceptable. But what are we to do? To back away from the plain intent of Jesus' words would be to redefine Christianity – and then it's no longer Christianity. In any case, society's preference for being inclusive cannot be held to apply to a matter of truth like this. How can truth ever be all-inclusive? If it is, then that leaves nothing to place in another category labelled 'error', and of course if there's no such thing as error, then there's no such thing as truth either. Jesus Christ said: "I am the Way, the Truth and the Life." It's a bit like saying 2 plus 2 equals 4, not 3 or 5, but 4, for that's the way it is – the 3 and the 5 are excluded from being the correct answer.

But someone says that may be what you believe is true, but it may not be the truth for other people. Sometimes they give an illustration of what they mean. They say, suppose a student is tied to a railway track for a prank. He should be okay because the approaching train is on the track alongside his, not the same one. But when the train whizzes by on the next line, the student has a heart attack and dies because he wasn't told that the train was on the other line. As far as he's concerned the train might as well have been on his line. He believed it was true, and so it became the truth for him.

In a similar way it's claimed that what's not true for me may actually become the truth as far as you are concerned. So, truth is supposed to be relative. In fact, we're told that there's no such thing as absolute truth. But this is nonsense! The objector is simply cheating with words! For, tell me, how can it be absolutely true that there's no such thing as absolute truth?! It can't, obviously, for that would be self-contradictory.

There are still those who think they've found an alternative way of salvation, or a religious counterpart to Jesus Christ, or else they may exclude themselves from Christ on account of their religious background – all of them holding these views very sincerely. But all the sincerity in the world can't change reality. We may cling to a system of beliefs which are very laudable in as far as they go - we say again we may be very sincere - but all the sincerity in the world can't alter objective truth. Reality doesn't oblige us by changing for us just because we want it to.

Jesus Christ is the truth and he, the Bible says, died for our sins and rose again. No-one else has done that. The truth about Jesus Christ is the all-important issue. It's a person's attitude to Christ that determines his or her eternal destiny. No matter the merits of other belief or value systems – and no matter how sincerely held – the truth is that God was in Jesus entering human history and fulfilling his plan of salvation, and except we believe that, we'll die in our sins (John 8:24). While it's true that we all have a right to believe what we like, we've all got to accept the consequences.

CHAPTER NINETEEN: AN APPEAL FROM COOKIES

Finally, let me tell you about a woman catching a flight at the airport. She's in a mad rush, and hasn't had time to eat on the way there; so she stops at the news stand to buy a pack of cookies, and then sits herself down at gate where there's a table between her and an older gentleman. But soon she can't believe her eyes when the man stretches over, picks up the pack of cookies from the table and helps himself to one. She's shocked, but doesn't want to make a scene so she just takes one herself, placing the pack back on the table – surely the man won't have the nerve to repeat his action! But he did, again he picks up the pack, looks at it thoughtfully, takes another cookie and after a little nibble, proceeds to gobble it up. By now she's pretty well hopping mad, how dare he just help himself to her cookies! Quickly she takes another herself – now there's just the one left.

Unbelievably, the chap reaches across again and picks out the last cookie, smiles at her, breaks it in half, and pushes the last half towards her. She's ready now to make a scene, but the boarding call comes and the chap jumps up and with another smile he's gone. At the gate the woman opens her bag to get her boarding pass and it's then she discovers her pack of cookies still in her bag – she'd been the one helping herself not him! The moral of that is that sometimes reality is a lot different from what we think – and we're in too much of a rush to check it out.

We have our misconceived ideas about where we come from; what the purpose of life is; and where we're going afterwards because we just feed on what society and the media around us tells us, all the time wrongly believing it to be the truth. I urge you to take a fresh look at things! Please check out whose bag of cookies you've been eating from!

Did you love *If Atheism Is True...?* Then you should read *Hope for Humanity: God's Fix for a Broken World* by Brian Johnston!

A conversational book, full of anecdotes and illustrations, yet direct and challenging - ideal to share the gospel or to strengthen and sharpen your own faith. Daily headlines remind us that this world is broken in so many different ways; an honest look within ourselves reveals deep problems too. This book pinpoints the same cause and the same solution – God's sending of His Son on a mission that would lead to a cross – with a challenge to every reader to accept or reject it.

Also by Brian Johnston

Search For Truth Bible Series
Healthy Churches - God's Bible Blueprint For Growth
Hope for Humanity: God's Fix for a Broken World
First Corinthians: Nothing But Christ Crucified
Bible Answers to Listeners' Questions

Standalone
Living in God's House: His Design in Action
Christianity 101: Seven Bible Basics
Nights of Old: Bible Stories of God at Work
A Test of Commitment: 15 Challenges to Stimulate Your
Devotion to Christ
John's Epistles - Certainty in the Face of Change
If Atheism Is True...

About the Author

Born and educated in Scotland, Brian worked as a government scientist until God called him into full-time Christian ministry on behalf of the Churches of God (www.churchesofgod.info). His voice has been heard on Search For Truth radio broadcasts for over 30 years during which time he has been an itinerant Bible teacher throughout the UK and Canada. His evangelical and missionary work outside the UK is primarily in Belgium and The Philippines. He is married to Rosemary, with a son and daughter.

About the Publisher

Hayes Press (www.hayespress.org) is a registered charity in the United Kingdom, whose primary mission is to disseminate the Word of God, mainly through literature. It is one of the largest distributors of gospel tracts and leaflets in the United Kingdom, with over 100 titles and hundreds of thousands despatched annually.

Hayes Press also publishes Plus Eagles Wings, a fun and educational Bible magazine for children, six times a year and Golden Bells, a popular daily Bible reading calendar in wall or desk formats.

Also available are over 100 Bibles in many different versions, shapes and sizes, Christmas cards, Christian jewellery, Eikos Bible Art, Bible text posters and much more!